# THE LOST LORE OF
# A MAN'S LIFE

*Wilderness Skills & Outdoor Arts*
*Recovered from Obscure Texts & Forgotten*
*Volumes of Advice & Information*
*for Modern Men & Boys,*
*with a Special Emphasis on the*
*Salubrious Effects of Life*
*as It Is Lived in Nature*

☞ **Clever & Entertaining Instruction from**
**One End of the Century to the Other**

☛ **How to Catch a Pig, Build a Fly-Fishing Rod,**
**Negotiate with Ducks & 1,000 Other Useful**
**and Interesting Facts**

# THE LOST LORE OF A MAN'S LIFE

## Lots of Cool Stuff Guys Used to Know but Forgot About the Great Outdoors

### All Stylishly Compiled by
### Denis Boyles, M.A.

Principal author of *A Man's Life: The Complete Instructions,*
*The Modern Man's Guide to Life, The Modern Man's Guide to*
*Modern Women,* and *Man Eaters Motel*

With Bibliographical Assistance from Gregg Stebben,
Who in Turn Was Aided by Karen Kriberney and a
Very Large Stack of Willowy Librarians

With Contributions from "Buzzacott," Col. Jas. A. Moss,
Stillman Taylor, Late Deputy Scout Commissioner R. F. McMurry,
Ernest Seton Thompson, Rolfe Cobleigh & Numerous Other
Sagacious Experts Now Sadly Departed

HarperPerennial
*A Division of* HarperCollins*Publishers*

HarperCollins books may be purchased for educational, business, or sales promotional use. For information please write: Special Markets Department, HarperCollins Publishers, Inc., 10 East 53rd Street, New York, NY 10022.

FIRST EDITION

*Designed by Interrobang Design Studio*

Library of Congress Cataloging-in-Publication Data

Boyles, Denis.
    The lost lore of a man's life : lots of cool stuff guys used to know but forgot about the great outdoors / by Denis Boyles with Gregg Stebben. — 1st ed.
       p.     cm.
    Includes index.
    ISBN 0-06-095224-5
    1. Outdoor life—Miscellanea.   2. Outdoor recreation—Miscellanea.   3. Men—Conduct of life.   I. Stebben, Gregg.  II. Title.
GV191.6.B69   1997
796.5—dc21                         97-9595

00  01  ❖/RRD 10 9 8

# Table of Contents

# Acknowledgments

∾⟋⟍∾

In addition to the authors of the books listed here, who supplied most of the contents of *Lost Lore of a Man's Life*, I'm also indebted to my cousin, Marvin, who let me use his extra house in town so I'd have someplace out of the rain to sit while I typed all this up. In addition, Deb, Carol, Kim, and all the smart and scenic women who work next door to Rex's pitched in to get this manuscript ready before the sheriff showed up. I'm also extremely grateful to Mauro DiPreta and Jennifer Griffin at HarperCollins. Jennifer was a guiding spirit of both Man's Life books. I owed her a thanks in the previous book, but I forgot. So here.

Of these authors, I'm most indebted to the redoubtable "Buzzacott," Francis Buzzacott, Col. Francis Buzzacott. He is by far the most relied-upon source for the information in this collection. There's a reason for that. Buzzacott is a man before my own heart; his outdoor books were not only extremely comprehensive, but were also unabashedly self-promoting. I certainly have absolutely no problem with that. In fact, where Buzzacott's editorial advertisements appeared, I simply substituted editorial advertisements of my own. I like to think Buzzacott would be happy knowing he's still out there promoting *somebody*.

Here's a modest bibliography of books recycled between these covers:

*Handy Farm Devices and How to Make Them*, Rolfe Cobleigh, New York, Orange Judd Company, 1913. By the way, I discovered after this manuscript was complete that this excellent compendium has just been reissued by Lyons & Burford.

*Farm Blacksmithing*, J.M. Drew, 2nd Ed., St. Paul, Minnesota, Webb Publishing Company, 1915

*The Complete American and Canadian Sportsman's Encyclopedia of Valuable Instruction*, Francis H. Buzzacott, Chicago, Press of R.R. Donnelley & Sons Co., 1905

*The Book of Woodcraft*, Ernest Thompson Seton, Garden City, New York, Garden City Publishing Co., Inc., 1912

*The Home Library of Entertainment, Instruction and Amusement*, Thomas Sheppard Meek, St. Louis, Mo., Thompson Publishing Co., 1902

*The Boy Mechanic* (Books One, Two and Three), Popular Mechanics Co., Chicago, Popular Mechanics Co. Publishers, Copyrighted 1913–1917 by H.H. Windsor

*The Boy Scouts Own Book*, edited by Franklin K. Mathiews, New York, D. Appleton and Company, 1915

*The Infantry Soldier's Hand Book*, Major William H. Waldron, New York, George U. Harvey, Inc., 1917

*Scouting*, National Headquarters Boy Scouts of America, New York, 1919

# ♦ ACKNOWLEDGMENTS ♦

This book was compiled at the commencement of William Jefferson Clinton's second term as President of the United States. In the spirit of these times, therefore, let me conclude with this obligatory statement:

In a book full of so much information, almost all of which has been gleaned from other sources, I'm pleased to say that I think I have been successful in weeding out errors and correcting mistakes. Where misinformation remains, however, I'm even more pleased to say the fault lies with the original authors: I didn't know about it, but if I had known about it, I wouldn't have permitted it. And above all, I had nothing personally to do with it.

Denis

# Compiler's Notice

Although I pocketed the money, almost every single one of the words in this book were written by somebody other than me. That in itself would make this book one of my own personal favorites. But there's more here: This book is made up of the best and most useful parts of many other books, all of which are also favorites of mine. Despite their undeserved obscurity, I felt these books also contained information that, if not exactly *lost,* had certainly been misplaced in our modern rush to make everything—including an overnight walk in the woods—an exercise in cutting edge technology. Instead of offering fuzzy advice of a radically alternative nature, these books all scream "Use common sense!" at top volume.

So think of this book as a kind of small attic filled with lots of old stuff that's still pretty good, all things considered. Maybe it will scare some guys to find out that some jobs are only done right one way. I mean, a man walks through the world today one foot in front of the other, much as he did a hundred years ago. The difference is that now the very act of walking is somehow suspect.

The focus in this book is on a man's life as it's lived outdoors, since, in my opinion, outdoors is the best place to see life unadorned. Outdoors is also a pretty exotic place for many modern men. From my own limited personal experience, I know there are TV producers and magazine editors in New York City, intimidating men on their own turf, who are terrified of the outdoors—especially if the outdoors is also *out of town.* For them, this book will constitute a kind of exotic travelogue. For the rest of us, it will contain familiar reassurances that what we thought was the right thing to do really was the right thing to do, after all.

Once again, my friend Gregg Stebben went through a huge pile of books, many of which were delivered to him by Karen Kriberney and by other librarians who are—or at least were—friends of hers. Now they are also friends of mine. There are additional acknowledgments elsewhere in this book.

This book is designed to fit neatly in your backpack or jacket pocket. It also snugs nicely on a shelf next to its big-brother book, *A Man's Life: The Complete Instructions.* It finds a resonance in the pages of *Men's Health* magazine, and at the encyclopedic Man's Life website located at http://www.manslife.com in the great wilderness of the World Wide Web. There is also the quarterly newspaper of *A Man's Life,* and, if you will write to the address below, I will always be happy to send you information about our fine stuff.

If you know of an old book full of useful information that you think I should know about, drop me a line or just stop by our friendly Office, where there is never a wait:

Real Life Publishing
c/o Rex's Barber Shop
116 West Jefferson St.,
Mankato, KS 66956
Telephone [913] 378–3772

Pass a note to old Rex and get a trim. You'll look much better by the time you leave.

Denis

# To Successfully Enjoy
# a Trip into the Woods

⌀▨▨⌀

What hat compels a man to leave hearth and home and venture into the embrace of Nature where danger and discomfort are the commonest forms of wildlife? It is nothing but a love for Creation and for all the creatures in it.

If you go out, travel light—but right. There's a great deal of difference in these words, just as much as between roughing it versus smoothing it. And if you follow these pages we shall endeavor to point out clearly to you the easiest way to obtain the right outfit, and to gain therefrom the fullest amount of comfort, pleasure, and benefit from a journey out-of-doors.

We omit nothing essential. We point out plainly how and what to provide, thus enabling you to provide for your every possible want, to live comfortably and well, and to receive from a minimum of cost and preparation a maximum of results from an outfit, simple in the extreme, yet one that with ordinary care will serve its purpose completely, and last you for many a long trip again besides.

## CAMP CLOTHING OUTFIT

See also our article on Camp Clothing and our advice in *A Man's Life: The Complete Instructions.*

For each person (sufficient for a month's trip or more):

1   suit of old serviceable woolen clothes.
1   extra pair of pants or overalls.
2   woolen or flannel overshirts.
2   suits of flannel underwear.
2   pair socks.
2   towels.
2   handkerchiefs.
1   featherweight rain cape.
1   empty pillowcase.
1   pair strong boots or shoes.
1   pair camp moccasins or slipper-shoes.
1   pair serviceable leggings.
1   broad-rim soft felt hat.
1   cape cap.
1   mosquito net.
1   woolen sweater.
1   pair suspenders.
1   ditty bag and contents (toilet articles, etc.).
1   combination camp bed, mattresses, blankets,
    and carry-all (four in one). (See Camp
    Combination.)

Wear part of the above and roll up the balance in carry-all as shown. Size of roll, 12 × 24 inches; weight, 15 pounds.

Carry on your person these items:

1   water cooling canteen.
1   reliable hunting knife.
1   waterproof safety match box (filled).
1   reliable pocket compass.
    A copy of this manual in your pocket.
    Pipe and tobacco if you smoke.
    Your gun or rod, if you hunt or fish.

## Suggestions in Camp Clothing.

Tan or Blue Flannel
Camping Shirt.

Type of Hunting Coat.

Campers' Rain
Coat Packed.

Featherweight Campers
Rain Cape.

Campaign Hat.
Drab Felt.

All Wool Camping or Hunting
Jacket. Khaki Color.

Summer Hat.

Summer Helmet.

Poncho Blanket
Cape.

Hunting Cap
and Cape.

All Wool Camping or
Hunting Sweater.
Khaki Color.

## The "Buzzacott" Army Mess Kit and Canteen.

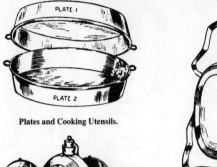

Plates and Cooking Utensils.

Method of Nesting.

Using the Cup.

Knife, Fork and Spoon.

Entire Kit Packed. (View of Cork.)

Bag.

# THE TENT

## Camp Cooking, Messing Outfit, Etc., Etc.
### *For Four Persons*

1 tent complete, with poles, guys, stakes, etc., 9 × 9 feet, 10-ounce khaki duck.

1 tent floor cloth to fit.

1 folding pocket axe.

1 tent fly, single or double (double preferred).

1 coil rope.

1 repair kit.

1 camp coffeepot.

3 camp stew or water kettles. (These combined form an excellent oven for baking or roasting.)

1 camp fry pan or skillet.

1 bake pan.

4 camp plates.

4 camp cups.

4 knives.

4 forks.

4 spoons.

1 salt and pepper dredge.

1 flask.

1 cook's spoon, large.

1 cook's fork, large.

1 cook's ladle dipper.

1 cook's turnover.

1 whetstone.

1 combination can opener and corkscrew.

1 campers manual with all camp cooking receipts.

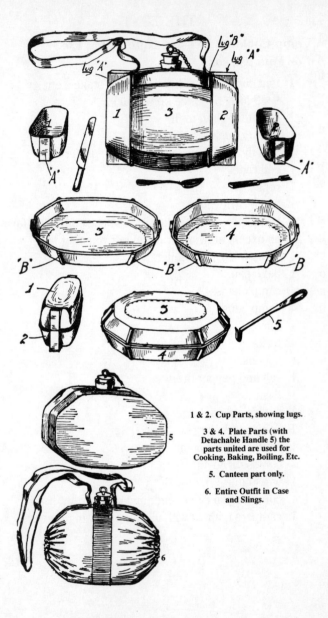

1 & 2.  Cup Parts, showing lugs.

3 & 4.  Plate Parts (with Detachable Handle 5) the parts united are used for Cooking, Baking, Boiling, Etc.

5.  Canteen part only.

6.  Entire Outfit in Case and Slings.

## The Simplest of All Camping Tents

The great trouble with camping-out tents is the weight of the frame, but the weight of the latter in the case of the tent figured herewith will hardly prove a burden to anyone, as only two light sticks are used, such as are shown in Figure 1.

These are pressed into the ground eight or ten feet apart, according to the size of the tent, and brought together and fastened at the upper ends with such a joint as is shown, or with a string passing through a screw-eye in each pole, if a simpler method is preferred.

The tent is made from four triangular pieces of cloth, as suggested in Figure 2. One of these is cut up the center and hemmed, to afford an entrance to the tent. The triangular pieces are sewed together at the edges, and at two of the opposite corners pieces of stout cord are sewed into the corners of the cloth, the cloth being reinforced as suggested in the cut.

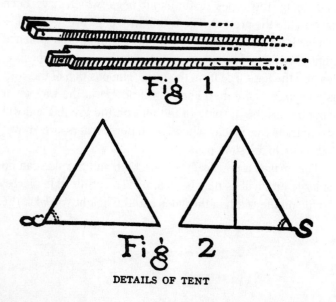

**Fig 1**

**Fig 2**

DETAILS OF TENT

**THE TENT SET UP**

Two stout pegs of wood and two lighter ones are provided. To pitch the tent, put up the two frame poles A-fashion and draw the tent cloth over them, opposite seams and corners fitting over the poles. Draw out the other two corners and tie by the ropes to the stout pegs, which have been driven into the ground. The two lighter pegs are used to fasten back the flaps of the front. It may be found well to hem a light cord into the bottom of the side having the opening, leaving the flaps free from the cord. The position of the cord is shown by the dotted line. It will not be in the way when lying across the opening of the tent on the ground and will strengthen the whole when the outer corners are drawn tightly up to the stout pegs.

This makes a practically square tent, and the size can be as large or small as may be desired. To cut the side pieces, decide on the width of the sides and the height you wish the tent to be. Then draw a triangle (Figure 2), having the base as long as desired for the side of the tent, and a perpendicular two feet longer than the height desired for the tent, since the four sides of the tent are to be inclined, and must, therefore, be enough longer to make up for this.

This will prove a very satisfactory tent for men who are camping out, and it has the merit of being easily made and very easy to carry about.

**To Heat a Tent Nights Without a Stove**—Build a campfire near tent opening, surround it partly with a radiator of logs, bark of tree, or brush, so as to throw the heat to inside.

**Another Way**—Throw into campfire a lot of stones, the larger the better, let them get red hot, put into bucket and carry into tent, invert the bucket over them, and it will surprise you. With a change of stones in the fire you can renew and keep warm all night long; or use camp kettle.

**Still Another Way**—(Perfectly safe if common sense is used.) Dig a pit half a bucket in size somewhere in tent. Fill it heaping full of red hot clear coals (embers) from the campfire, taking care no unburnt or smoky wood is therein. Now cover this with the kettle or pail. With mud, plaster up the edges, and it will keep your tent and you warm all night long. Use camp pails (iron of course).

**In Case of Fire in Tent**—If serious, lay hold of the bottom of the bedding and pull out, and with a blanket smother the fire quickly. If fire is caught in time you can smother it.

Let the tent go, but save the outfit therein, if possible. You can improvise shelter but not the outfit, so save that part first.

# CAMP RATIONS

## Four Men—Five Days or More

### United States Standard Ration Scale (ample without any allowance for fish, game, etc.): Quantity and Variety Larger (quality the very best)

20 lbs. self-rising flour.
6 lbs. fresh biscuits.
6 lbs. Indian or cornmeal.
6 lbs. select navy beans.
3 lbs. select special rice.
5 lbs. select salt pork.
5 lbs. select choice bacon.
10 lbs. select fine ham.
15 lbs. new potatoes.
6 lbs. fresh onions.
1 3-lb. can preserved butter.
3 lbs. dried fruits.
½ gallon pickles in vinegar.
1 quart syrup.
1 box pepper.
1 box mustard.
½ gallon preserves.
6 lbs. choice mixed coffee.
6 lbs. choice sugar.
½ lb. mixed tea.
½ lb. baking powder.
½ lb. baking soda.
6 boxes matches, tin case.
1 lb. soap.
1 lb. cornstarch.
1 lb. candies.
4 cans milk and cream.
1 sack salt.

1 jar cheese.
1 box ginger.
1 box allspice.
1 lb. currants.
1 lb. raisins.
6 boxes sardines.
1 screwtop flask.
All packed in airtight or tin packages.
Total weight, 125 pounds.

In addition to the above we suggest that you carry ready for immediate use this book, fresh bread, meat, sausage, or a few eggs in case (to last for first day or two only)—all about the size of your bandanna handkerchief full.

*Thus stand we prepared for all things.*

## CAMP LIFE

Camping is simple life reduced to actual practice, as well as the culmination of the outdoor life.

Camping has no great popularity today because men have the idea that it is possible only after an expensive journey to the wilderness; and women that it is inconvenient, dirty, and dangerous.

These are errors. They have arisen because camping as an art is not understood. When intelligently followed, camp life must take its place as a cheap and delightful way of living, as well as a mental and physical savior of those strained or broken by the grind of the overbusy world.

The wilderness affords the ideal camping, but many of the benefits can be got by living in a tent on a town lot, a piazza, or even a housetop.

**The Magic of the Campfire.** What is a camp without a campfire? No camp at all, but a chilly place in a landscape, where some people happen to have some things.

When first the brutal anthropoid stood up and walked erect—this was man, and the great event was symbolized and marked by the lighting of the first campfire.

For millions of years our race has seen in this blessed fire the means and emblem of light, warmth, protection, friendly gathering, council. All the hallow of ancient thoughts, hearth, fireside, home is centered in its glow, and the home tie itself is weakened with the waning of the home fire. Not in the steam radiator can we find the spell; not in the water coil; not even in the gas log; they do not reach the heart. Only the ancient sacred fire of wood has power to touch and thrill the chords of primitive remembrance. When men sit together at the campfire they seem to shed all modern form and poise, and hark back to the primitive—to meet as man and man—to show the naked soul. Your campfire partner wins your inner love; and having camped in peace together, is a lasting bond of union—however wide your worlds may be apart.

The campfire, then, is the focal center of all primitive brotherhood. We shall not fail to use its magic powers.

**Woodcraft Pursuits.** Realizing that *manhood,* not *scholarship,* is the first aim of education, we have sought out those pursuits that develop the finest character, the finest physique, and that may be followed out of doors, which, in a word, *make for manhood* and may be begun at any time, regardless the age of the man—or boy.

By nearly every process of logic we are led primarily to

Woodcraft—that is, Woodcraft in a large sense—meaning every accomplishment of an all-around woodsman—riding, hunting, camp-craft, scouting, mountaineering, Indian-craft, first aid, star-craft, signaling, and boating. To this we add all good outdoor athletics and sports, including sailing and motoring, and nature study, of which wild animal photography is an important branch; but above all, Heroism.

**Honors by Standards.** The competitive principle is responsible for much that is evil. We see it rampant in our colleges today, where every effort is made to discover and develop a champion, while the great body of students is neglected. That is, the ones who are in need of physical development do not get it, and those who do not need it are overdeveloped. The result is much unsoundness of many kinds. A great deal of this would be avoided if we strove to bring all the individuals up to a certain standard. On our non-competitive test the enemies are not "the other fellows" but time and space, the forces of Nature. We try not to down the others, but to raise ourselves. A thorough application of this principle would end many of the evils now demoralizing college athletics. Therefore, all our honors are bestowed according to worldwide standards.

**A Heroic Ideal.** The boy from ten to fifteen, like the savage, is purely physical in his ideals. I do not know that I ever met a boy that would not rather be John L. Sullivan than Darwin or Tolstoi. Therefore, I accept the fact, and seek to keep in view an ideal that is physical, but also clean, manly, heroic, already familiar, and leading with certainty to higher things.

—Ernest Seton Thompson

### How to Break Large Sticks of Firewood

If you wish to break a large piece of firewood, and you have no hand ax, the following method may often be used: Place your stick in the crotch of a tree (X), B-C equaling the length you wish broken off.

Then grasp the stick at A and pull backwards. The pressure at B is so great that the stick is broken there. The longer A-B the more pressure, and therefore the greater likelihood of the stick breaking.

## A ONE-DAY HIKE

It is a good rule in hiking never to set out with the determination that you are going to show how *hardy* you are. It is as bad as setting out to show how *smart* you are. "Smart Aleck" always lands in the gutter. Do not set out to make a record. Record breakers usually come to grief in the end. Set out on your hike determined to *be moderate*. That is, take a *few* fellows; not more than a dozen. Plan a *moderate trip,* of which not more than half the time must be consumed in going and coming.

These are some rules found good in hiking:

- Do not go in new shoes.
- Be sure your toenails and corns are well pared before going.
- Do not take any very little or weak fellows.

- Be prepared for rain.
- Take a pair of dry socks.
- Travel Indian file in woods, and double Indian file on roads.
- Always have with you a rule and tape line, knife, some string, and some matches.
- Take a compass, and sometimes a pocket level.
- Take a map, preferably the topographical survey.
- Take a notebook and pencil.
- Do not waste time over things you can do as well, or better, at home.

And last, and most important,

- It is wise to *set out with an object*. Read on.

Here are samples of objects for a short hike in winter:

- To determine that hard maple (or other timber) does or does not grow in such woods.
- To prove that a certain road runs north and south.
- To decide whether the valley is or is not higher than the one across the divide.
- To prove that this or that hill is higher than such a one.
- To get any winter fungi.
- To look for evergreen fern.
- To get, each, 100 straight rods, 30 inches long, to make Indian bed, of willow, hazel, kinnikinnik, arrowroot, etc.
- If there is snow, to take, by the tracks, a census of a given woods, making full-size drawings of each track—that is, four tracks, one for each foot; and also give the distance to the next set.
- If there is snow, to determine whether there are any skunk dens in the woods, by following every skunk

trail until it brings you to its owner's home.

- Now, be it remembered that any one who sticks to a plan, merely because he started that way, when it turns out to be far from the best, is not only unwise, he is stupid and obstinate.

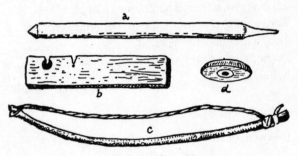

1. Tools for firemaking

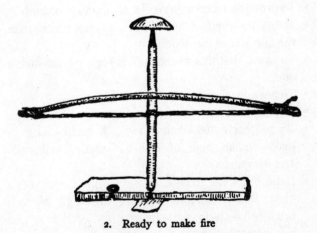

2. Ready to make fire

# CAMPING FIRES

## Starting a Fire by Rubbing Together Sticks

Take a piece of dry, sound, balsam-fir wood (or else cedar, cypress, tamarac, basswood, or cottonwood, in order of choice) and make of it a drill and block, thus:

*Drill.* Five-eighths of an inch thick, 12 to 15 inches long; roughly rounded, sharpened at each end as in the cut.

*Block, or board,* 2 inches wide, 6 or 8 inches long, ⅝ inch thick. In this block, near one end, cut a side notch one-half an inch deep, wider on the underside; and near its end half an inch from the edge make a little hollow or pit in the top of the block.

*Tinder.* For tinder use a wad of fine, soft, very dry, dead grass mixed with shredded cedar bark, birch bark, or even cedar wood scraped into a soft mass.

*Bow.* Make a bow of any bent stick two feet long, with a strong buckskin or belt-lacing thong on it.

*Socket.* Finally, you need a socket. This simple little thing is made in many different ways. Sometimes I use a pine or hemlock knot with a pit ¼ inch deep, made by boring with the knife point. But it is a great help to have a good one made of a piece of smooth, hard stone or marble, set in wood; the stone or marble having in it a smooth, round pit ⅜ inch wide and ⅜ inch deep. The one I use most was made by the Eskimo.

Now, we are ready to make the fire:

Under the notch in the fire-block set a thin chip.

Turn the leather thong of the bow once around the drill: The thong should now be quite tight. Put one point of the drill into the pit of the block, and on the upper end put the socket, which is held in the left hand, with the top of the drill in the hole of the stone. Hold the left wrist against the left shin, and the left foot on the fire-block. Now, draw the right hand back and forth steadily on level and the *full length* of the bow. This causes the drill to twirl in the pit. Soon it bores in, grinding out powder, which presently begins to smoke. When there is a great volume of smoke from a growing pile of black powder, you know that you have the spark. Cautiously lift the block, leaving the smoking powder on the chip. Fan this with your hand till the live coal appears. Now, put a wad of the tinder gently on the spark; raise the chip to a convenient height, and blow till it bursts into flame.

1. *The notch must reach the middle of the firepit.*
2. You must hold the *drill steadily* upright, and cannot do so without bracing the left wrist against the left chin, and having the block on a firm foundation.
3. You must begin lightly and slowly, pressing heavily and *sawing fast after there is smoke.*
4. *If the fire does not come, it is because you have not followed these instructions.*

—Ernest Seton Thompson

## How to Build a Conventional Camping Fire and Use It Right

Select two medium thick green logs and level off the tops with the camp axe as shown in the engraving.

Set and brace these logs a few inches apart, only so as they will form support on which the bottom of your utensil will rest safely; scrape out a little trench underneath and with a few pieces more form the windguard or radiator shown in the illustration, and your splendid camp range is complete.

Here can be easily accomplished, with care, all the known culinary arts, even without utensils; take note of this fact; even roasting, baking, broiling, etc., and should your outfit be such as this manual designates, no dish known to mankind need be slighted one jot.

An improvised shelter can be made over this proof against sun or rain and which will be useful also for the preservation of meats, fish, and game, as these pages will later show.

With such simple arrangements as these even the fire need never go out; neither will it be necessary to burn fuel by the acre nor to chop any wood; thus can you save your exertions and the axe for more fitting purposes.

## To Use a Fire Properly

As to the amount of fire to get the most results from: You will find it right to utilize only the flame at one end for your boiling and stewing. The hot ashes or live coals only should be used for frying, boiling, baking, roasting, etc., not so much for economy of wood as for less danger of burning, spilling, etc.

If this advice is followed very little smoke is the result. If anything looks amateur-like, it is to see one cooking over a big, roaring, smoky campfire, large and hot enough to roast an ox.

If the fire is handled right, there need be no more smoke than would fill the cook's hat, much less than make him choke and gasp like most do.

Let the wood smoke and the fire burn (just before you commence the cooking), then when ready your live coals will give you even more heat than you require for any small party. (Old camp cooks take out unburnt wood before they start cooking—the greenhorn puts on more wood and it makes him suffer accordingly for his ignorance.)

Keep wood dry by stacking it up and should rain fall your wood is fairly dry and your camp neat besides.

## CAMP COOKING RECEIPTS

**Camp Coffee**—(2 cups for each person). To every cup of water allow a tablespoonful of ground coffee; then last, add one for pot. Put in cold water and set on to boil. Allow to boil up just once; remove from fire; settle with ¼ cup cold water and serve piping hot.

**Another Way**—Bring water to boiling point first; add coffee, boil five minutes, settle and serve. A good way is to put the coffee in a small muslin bag, tied loose; then boil five minutes longer and your bag of grounds can be removed before serving.

**Camp Tea**—Teaspoonful of tea to each person, one for pot. Pour over fresh boiling water; set aside in warm place for ten minutes to steep, then serve. (Don't boil good fresh tea.) Boil old tea leaves three minutes for second serving and you have as good tea as the first; try it, then wash out pot and burn the leaves in campfire.

**Substitute for Coffee**—Parched barley, beans, rice, and bread crumbs make a fair substitute; scorch a trifle and grind. You can improvise a coffee mill with a bag and stone, pounding the coffee fine.

A supply of "Horlick's Malted Milk" in chocolate tablet form is an excellent substitute for coffee or tea. It is food and drink—and a hearty and substantial meal can be made from them. Twenty-five tablets make a good meal and a screw tip flask holds 75 to 100 of them and can be used for liquids when empty.

**Camp Yeast or Ranchmen's Bread**—This is a most simple and effective way of making splendid bread or biscuit for the permanent camp and is much easier to the inexperienced than it seems. If your camp is for a week in one place we suggest a thorough trial. If you succeed you will teach the wife later on.

Take a common lard pail or any covered small bucket, and mix a simple batter of flour, warm water, a pinch of salt, and a spoonful of sugar; about a quart in all. Cover this and set aside in a warm but not hot place; one side of the fire will do. When it lifts the cover of the pail (which it will surely do unless tied down) it is ready for use.

You will now note that this quart of flour has raised to the top of the kettle by fermentation and is now excellent yeast.

Take nearly all of this—saving say ¼ for next baking—and knead it into sufficient flour to make a good stiff bread dough. This you can knead all you wish—only not too stiff—roll it out and add to it a spoonful of camp lard, sugar, and a teaspoonful of baking soda. Knead again, form into thin biscuits or bread, put in oven, set in the warm until it raises to double size, then bake until done.

You now have as delicious a biscuit as your baker ever turned out.

Into balance of sourdough or yeast batter stir more flour and set aside until ready for more baking. This is genuine rancher's bread used universally on the plains. The only essential to its success is care and warmth.

**Fried Bacon**—Slice and soak half hour (if very salt) in water, if not, lay slices as cut in hot pan on the ashes of the fire. Fry until brown on both sides and serve.

**Camp Biscuits**—Use self-rising flour; if not, to a quart of flour add small tablespoonful baking powder, large pinch of salt, and tablespoonful camp lard (bacon fat), make dough soft with cold water and stir with a spoon, just enough to make a fairly stiff dough. Do not knead or stir too much as this makes heavy biscuits. Drop from spoon into well-greased pan or kettle, biscuit size, and bake in oven fifteen minutes or until well browned and done.

**Biscuits, Bread, Etc., to Test When Done**—Run a dry sliver of thin hard wood into center; if dough sticks to sliver when you pull it out continue baking more until sliver will come out clean and dry, then your biscuit or bread will be well done.

Don't think you must have a range or stove to have a good oven. As good an oven as can be built is made by the simple plan of taking two sufficiently large plates—common baking pans or stew kettles; one a trifle larger than the other, so as to be inverted over each other easily; fit them first so as to be sure of the right ones.

Into the smaller set your bread, biscuits, meats, game, fish, or whatever you desire to bake or roast; now make near your campfire a flat, good thick bed of coals (embers from the fire); on it place your pan or kettle containing the food, with the large one inverted over it. Strew more live coals on its top and you have a most excellent oven—one that needs no attention except when roasting meats and then only to renew the fire coals when burnt out or needed; otherwise it need not be touched until it is done; ready to serve. If roasting, basting is unnecessary. Allow fifteen minutes for biscuits; bread, fifteen to twenty minutes; meats, one to two hours according to size; beans, three to six hours, if possible.

By above plan anything can be excellently roasted, even well-browned, perfect. *(See also Camp Oven Without Utensils.)*

**Slap Jacks**—A simple batter of flour, etc., thinner than biscuit dough, so it will run thick, drop in small quantities into hot pan, well greased, fry brown, turn over. Brown and fry fairly dry. If made right they are far more substantial than cake; sprinkled when hot with sugar they are excellent and stick to the ribs on a long tramp. As a bacon sandwich for lunch they are fine.

> It is an excellent plan to utilize only the embers of a campfire for baking, roasting, frying, or broiling and to conduct these operations on one side of the fire only. The direct flame of campfire should be only used on pots, kettles, etc.

**Stale Bread and Biscuits** can be made fresh by wrapping in damp cloth and placing in oven for a few minutes. Very stale bread is excellent if dipped once in salt water and fried brown in bacon fat.

**Camp Bread**—Made same as biscuits only in a loaf form. It should be flattened out to fully cover the size of oven. In either case grease well the oven bottom or dredge the bottom of dough with flour to prevent sticking.

**Soda Biscuits**—Small teaspoonful soda, pinch of salt, and spoonful of camp lard into quart of flour, mix as for biscuits, and bake. Use only one-half as much soda as baking powder or they will turn yellow and taste bitter. *(See also Bread Without Oven, etc., etc.)*

**Broiled Small Birds**—Clean and parboil them first, then broil over hot clean embers of the fire using a split as shown on page 00. Excellent for broiling any kinds of meats.

**Corn or Johnnycakes**—One-half flour, one-half meal, mix not as stiff as biscuit dough; pour into pan or kettle and bake slowly thirty minutes or until done.

The tendency of most camp cooks is to have too much fire.

> See Campfire Observations, etc.

**Pork Fritters**—Slice salt pork, soak, and roll in meal or flour. Drop in hot fat and fry brown.

**Fried Fish, Game, Etc.**—Clean well; season and fry as above. Always fry in hot fat; it sears the outside and retains the juices and flavor, while to put meats on in cold pan and fat extracts juices and makes good meat tough. Don't salt fresh meats before frying; salt in pan, when nearly done, before serving.

**Fried Potatoes**—Slice and fry raw potatoes in hot fat. Brown both sides, season with salt as you remove them, serve red hot.

If sliced boiled potatoes, use but little fat, season with salt and pepper while cooking and brown in pan.

Good seasoning is one-half of good cooking. Don't guess at it, season to taste.

**Boiled Potatoes**—If new potatoes, don't put on in cold water; drop in boiling water instead; put in small handful of salt. When you can easily pierce them with a fork or sliver they are done. Strain well; dry a minute over fire and serve.

If old potatoes, soak for half hour, just put them on in cold water. Boil such potatoes with skins on, after washing twice, slicing piece off each end; guess what for.

**Baked or Roast Potatoes**—Wash and dry well; bury deep in good live coals—ashes of fires; cover well with hot coals until well done.

**Roast Meats, Game, Etc.**—Clean and prepare; dredge well with flour, pepper, etc., a little salt, add a few sliced onions and a slice or two of bacon or salt pork on top for basting qualities. Add a little boiling water to start the gravy; then it is ready for pan or pot roast.

See also Cooking Without Utensils, Oven, etc.

**Fried Mush**—Slice cold, boiled mush. Roll in flour and fry in hot pan with little fat. Cornmeal requires much cooking—boil and stir for twenty to thirty minutes.

**Soups, Stews, Etc.**—Crack fresh bones into pieces, add meats, scraps, and a slice or so of bacon or pork, cover with cold water, and boil slowly until meat is well done; then add onions and a few teaspoonfuls rice or cooked beans. Boil until done, slowly; season to taste.

**Meats for Soups, Etc.**—Should be put on in cold water and simmered slowly—always. Allow boiled meats, hams especially, to cool off in the water they are boiled in—they slice better—are tender and there is a big difference all around.

**Camp Pudding**—Have ready a large kettle of boiling water—plenty of it—and a large bag made from a piece of flour sack; dip the bag into the boiling water and dredge flour on the inside of bag. Cut into dice-size pieces one cup of fat and salt-pork; toll in flour to separate the mass, then to three cups flour add one cup sugar; one cup currants; two teaspoonfuls spice. If desired dried fruit cut in small pieces can be used in lieu of currants. Add water to this and stir into good thick paste or batter. Turn this out into floured cloth—allow room for swelling of pudding to double its size; tie up tight in cloth; drop in boiling water and boil for two hours. Don't let the water stop boiling or your pudding will spoil—better have a little extra so as to allow for boiling away. Use no baking powder or soda. Just try it once!

**Sauce for Above**—One-quarter cup sugar; two teaspoonfuls of spice, cup of evaporated cream or water. Mix cold and heat over fire to boiling point, stirring well; remove from fire and stir in a teaspoonful or more vinegar to taste. The vinegar will give it a flavor like brandy sauce—just try it, following directions exactly.

**Rice Pudding**—Put cupful of rice in plenty water, a little salt; don't be afraid of too much water; boil until a grain can be mashed easily between thumb and first finger, then pour off water or strain through cloth. Every grain of this rice will be whole and separate if done correctly as above. To this rice add a cup of sugar, a spoonful of spices, and a cup of currants. If possible a little condensed milk and water—say a cupful. Set aside in warm place—not over fire—for fifteen minutes, until liquid is absorbed and you have rice pudding.

> It is well to note that in this "Camp Cookery" we have no receipts except what conform to the contents of our Ration Chest, and if they are carefully followed we vouch for surprising results. The receipts herein have been tested for years by many thousands who have used this manual (depended on it) exclusively.

**Camp Pot Pie**—Simply follow receipts for soups or stews, only leave out the bones. Fifteen minutes before serving drop in by the teaspoonful a cup of ordinary biscuit dough. Put on cover and boil until done. Boil slowly and not so as to burn. Add sliced potatoes and onions also.

**Don't boil meat fast, it toughens it.**

**Smoked Herrings** toasted or broiled over campfire are excellent.

**Boiled Beans**—Always soak beans overnight if possible using double water and allowing room to swell (a pint of dried beans makes a quart or more). If you can't soak them put on in cold water with a piece of pork or bacon—say a pound therein; when it boils add a teaspoonful of baking soda; boil until beans are well done, adding more water if necessary. Season to taste with salt and pepper, a few spoonfuls of sugar, one of mustard. Pot beans should cook thus, three hours or more.

**Baked Beans**—Simply take the above; arrange them in oven (which see) or you can use preserve jar if empty. Score the top of bacon or pork; press into center; cover with hot water and bake from one to three hours more (an onion adds to flavor). The longer a bean is cooked the better it is. *(See also Cooking Without Utensils.)*

A teaspoonful of baking soda makes hard water soft—try it when boiling beans.

**Leaky Utensils** will be better for an application of soap or a paste made of flour, salt, and fine wood ashes plastered on and dried. Cracks in stoves and ranges can be cemented by the above most effectively by leaving out the flour.

**Camp Meat or Game Pie**—Line a kettle with a pie crust of the following: To a quart of water add a teaspoonful of salt, ¼ teaspoonful of pepper, and a cup of camp lard, add a layer of cooked meats or game (after removing the bones), then a layer of onions, then a layer of potatoes until kettle is nearly full, over this lay a thin sheet of the pie crust and pinch the edges together, cut a slit in center of top and pour in one pint of boiling water, and bake for one-half hour slowly or until crust and vegetables are well done. Roll out crust with a bottle.

**Camp Stew**—Use raw meats or game and stew slowly until very well done, then add vegetables and stew again until they are done, season to taste, thicken ten minutes before serving with two spoonsful of flour batter.

**Camp Cookies or Hotcakes**—To a quart of flour add a tablespoonful of baking powder or one teaspoonful of baking soda and a pinch of salt, mix well, then add a cup of currants or chopped dried fruit, a cup of syrup or sugar, teaspoonful of mixed spices, two teaspoonfuls of camp lard, mix with cold water to a thick batter, roll out, cut into round cakes, using baking powder can cover as a cake cutter, and bake in quick hot oven fifteen minutes; watch the baking.

**Rich Soup and Gravy Coloring**—Tablespoonful burnt sugar or flour—rich brown.

**Fish Chowder**—Cut small slices of pork or bacon—fry them out in kettle, then put in layer of fish cut in slices on the pork or bacon thus fried—then a layer of onions and then potatoes and biscuit and repeat in layers as above until all materials are in. Season each successive layer, cover with water, and stew slowly for half an hour or until well done.

**Use Meat Water**—Water that meats have been boiled in for pea or bean soups.

**Cornbread**—One quart cornmeal, teaspoonful salt, one of baking powder or soda, mix with cold water to a thin batter, set to rise—when ready to bake stir your batter well, and put into bake pan or oven and bake slowly for half an hour or more until well done. In making corn mush, use a paddle whittled from a stick; stir often and cook well thirty to forty-five minutes slowly.

**Gingerbread**—Three cups flour, one cup of molasses, one-half cup of lard or camp fat, two teaspoonfuls of ginger, one teaspoonful of baking soda, water to make a thick batter; stir well and bake in hot oven.

**Salt Meat Stew**—Take a few slices of salt pork or bacon, soak in water for half an hour, then place them in pot and partially fry them; add sliced onions, potatoes, and biscuits in layers and season to taste. Stew slowly until done, adding just enough water to barely cover the stew; thicken with flour or meal if desired fifteen minutes before serving.

**Fish Cakes**—Take cold fish and remove the bones; mince well with equal parts of bread crumbs and potatoes; season well and fry in little fat. Brown well both sides. An onion helps it.

> Always carry on a long trip a water canteen and a lunch in your haversack; a slapjack and bacon sandwich is fine. (It will not dry up or crumble to pieces.)

# SAMPLE DAY'S CAMP MENU

**Bill of Fare**

**BREAKFAST**

Hot Wheat and Corn Cakes (Flap Jacks), Syrup

Pork Fritters or Fried Bacon and Potatoes

Camp Bread          Preserves          Hot Coffee

**DINNER**

Camp Baked Pork and Beans

Baked Potatoes          Pickles

Coffee          Bread

Plum, Rice, or Bread Pudding

**SUPPER**

Hot Soda Biscuit          Camp Pot Pie

Hot Tea          Cheese          Crackers

*(Taken from the ration list only.)*

The variety of our camp rations and camp cooking receipts suffice to give a daily change of menu for each day in the week.

## COOKING WITHOUT UTENSILS (FOR EMERGENCY CASES)

See also Utensils and How to Make.

**Bread of Scones**—Can be baked by using a large thin stone well heated first in campfire, then placed on embers near fire. Flatten out dough to cover the stone, turn when underpart will permit until done. Scones are equal parts of meal, bran, or flour.

**Frog Legs and Mushrooms**—Make a dainty camp dish and are often found around camp—look out for the wrong kind; toadstools, they are poisonous. Mushrooms show a pink or brown underneath and peel easy, while toadstools are black or white underneath and do not peel easy; if you are not sure of the difference, do not eat them. You may need an emetic. *(See Camp Doctor below.)*

**Bread, Without Stone Even**—Make a good, stiff dough adding a little more salt, but no lard; pull it out into a long thin strip, wrap this corkscrew-like on a stick of wood with bark on (tree branch). Hold over very hot fire of ashes (not flame) turning constantly until done. Try this pulled for bread—it's great!

**For Large Game,** wild turkeys, etc. Wrap in common clay and bury in pit of coals all night; in the morning take it out, break off case; feathers, skin, etc., will fall off with it and you will try this many a time thereafter.

**Well-Soaked or Cooked Beans**—Place in bucket, kettle, or pot; covered with water and buried in pit of coals all night as above, are cooked in the morning. Cover kettle, of course.

**Roast Meats, Fish, Game, Etc.—Without Utensils**— Clean fish or game thoroughly, place on piece of green bark of tree. Wrap it all up in green grass; bury in pit full of red hot live coals (no unburnt wood); red-hot ashes are best; for two hours or more according to size. When done remove outside skin and serve. Another way is to roll in soaked paper instead of dried grass.

Fish or feathered game need not have scales or feathers removed; simply wet them before covering; when done, skin. Scales or feathers will all come off together easily and the delicious flavor of the flesh will taste as you never tasted it before. Season after it is done to taste.

**Frying or Broiling Without Utensils**—Use the green, thick bark of a tree, rough side down on fire. Use the campfire tongs (as illustrated elsewhere) or make a toaster and broiler as shown, from a stick having a split end which will hold the meat over a hot coal fire. Don't pierce the meat.

Always carry a small bag of salt in the haversack

**To Roast Whole Game—Open Campfire**—Note above spit and forked sticks; turn constantly. Large game requires two men to turn right. Excellent for rib roasts or large game.

A little charcoal (burnt wood) thrown into a pot with slightly tainted meats will sweeten them.

Scour pots, pans, and kettles immediately on emptying contents before they cool off (they clean twice as easy and well). Use sand and water; It is far better than soap.

**Greens**—Carefully picked spring dandelions make an excellent mess of greens for a camp. Boil in salted water (like spinach) until tender, changing water twice.

**To Preserve Meats, Fish, Game, Etc.**—Slice meat to be preserved in long thin slices, knead plenty of salt in and lay covered aside so as to absorb salt for four hours. Then spread out singly in the hot sun to dry for a few days, or smoke well for twenty-four hours over a good thick smoke, on a frame of green twigs. When properly cured they are dry to the touch and have shrunk up to one half their size. This is sun-dried or smoked jerked meat, so universally used on the plains by both white men and Indians alike. Fish can be cured the same way. Turn skin side up or remove skin when removing bones.

Meats cured carefully by this method will last for a year or more; eat raw or fry.

---

### To Build a Camp Oven

Dig a hole in the ground about 18 inches square and 4 inches deep. Invert a bucket in this, or, if this is unavailable, build a frame of sticks and thatch it with mud, leaving a small square hole in the end for a door. A fire is then built all around the oven and, when it is hot, food, bread, or whatever is to be baked, may be placed inside. Such an oven will bake bread almost as well as the one at home.

—Scout Cyril Norman, N.C.

---

### A Convenient Way of Cooking

Build your fire between two logs or stones, on which can be placed a grate from an oven, which must, of course, be brought from home beforehand. In this way several articles may be cooked at the same time, without danger of spilling the contents into the fire. Fine toast may be made also over the hot coals.

## MISCELLANEOUS HINTS AND POINTERS ON CAMPING

**A Hot Sweat Bath**—Can be arranged in camp with hot stones and a little water sprinkled on them after first covering yourself and the stones with blankets. A frame may also be constructed to make a more commodious facility. This is the Indian method of curing most all complaints.

**Camp Lantern (Fish and Game Snare)**—Take a piece of phosphorous (walnut size), submerge it in a saucer of water and cut into little pieces, then put into small bottle with two ounces sweet oil, cork tightly, tie to a limb or stick. Stuck into the ground, it attracts game at night, or if tied to a string and dropped into the water where fish abound it will attract their attention and they can be caught.

**A Good Camp Lamp**—Can be made by using clear tallow fat (fat of animals), melted down and put in an old tin can. Improvise a wick from unraveled cotton or tent canvas, put one end in can and the other end on edge of can and wire.

**A Good Camp Candlestick**—A safe one can be improvised from a potato with a hole in it—bottom sliced off so it will stand firmly—or an old can partly filled with dirt.

**A Good Camp Spoon, Knife, and Fork**—Can be made from a shell and split stick. A fork can easily be whittled, and a good knife made from a piece of tin cut from an old can and inserted in a split stick; lash it tight with wire.

**A Good Dinner Plate or Cooking Utensil,** from a piece of green thick barky tree, using smooth part for food.

**Any Old Tin Can**—Top carefully burnt out over campfire, then scoured, makes a good cup or small cooking utensil.

**To Keep Matches Dry**—Cork a few in a small bottle. *(See also Waterproof Matchboxes.)*

**To Correctly Ascertain the Point of the Compass**—Face the sun in the morning; spread out your arms straight from the body—before you is the east, behind you is the west, to your right hand, the south, left, north, (accurately). If the sun don't shine, note the tops of pine trees; they invariably dip to the north. *(See also Lost in Camp.)*

**A Reliable Camp Clock**—A very accurate one can be improvised by making a sundial of a piece of stick stuck in the earth where the sun's rays can cast the shadow of the stick on the ground. You can mark the ground most accurately if one of your party has a watch. Then the clock will serve you well when the man with the watch is gone. It will not vary like a watch and will tell the time correctly when the watch won't; don't forget that.

**A Whetstone** is handier and more useful than a butcher's steel. It can be used for exactly the same purpose anyway, and will sharpen the axe and all tools when a steel will not.

**Don't Spoil a Good Knife**—In opening tin cans in camp; take the camp axe. Cut across in the center and open the cuts afterward, but not with the fingers.

---

### To Keep Warm at Night

I went to a harness shop and bought six blanket pins. They are large safety pins, and are sold two for a nickel, but can only be gotten at harness stores at this price. They are willing to sell any number. I take the pins with me on my hikes and use them to pin the bedding down around the edges to prevent it from getting disarranged during the night. On these chilly evenings, it is not very pleasant to awake and find your foot out in the dew! If the pin is stuck through twice, or made to come out on the same side it went through first, there will be no danger of the bedclothes being torn. I have used less than six at a time, but six is a good number.

This is very simple, but is a great help to my scouts and myself. I always take several extra pins along to supply the "first nighters," and to sell to those wishing them.

—Scoutmaster Rollo C. Hester, Indiana

---

**To Find Out Correctly How the Winds Blow**—If the wind is very light, place your finger in your mouth for a minute, moisten it, then hold it in the air. The coolest side indicates the direction from which the wind blows.

**How to Catch Frogs**—You can catch frogs with hook and line baited with red or scarlet rag (it's like shaking red cloth at a bull). Clean the hindquarters and roll in meal or flour and fry in hot fat. They are delicious.

**A Good Fire Shovel**—Can be made of a piece of tin and split stick; it is also an excellent broiler.

**Paper Insulation**—Sheets of paper, or an old newspaper sewed between two blankets, equals three blankets. A thin vest lined with paper equals two.

**Comfortable Underwear**—If the seams of underwear chafe or gall the skin, turn inside out. Common cornstarch is a most excellent talcum or chafing preventative and cure. (It's in our ration list.)

**If Soaking Wet**—If soaking wet and no dry clothes handy take off wet garments and wring them out as dry as possible—put on again—you are less liable to take cold, and will be much warmer besides.

**Don't Sleep**—Don't sleep with the moon shining on your face, you can get moonstruck, and it's as bad almost as a sunstroke.

**Burn Up All Kitchen and Table Refuse**—Even potato skins and wet tea or coffee grounds; burn out even tin cans in the campfire; if thrown out they are fly and maggot breeders, and mean lots of flies in camp. Burnt out and thrown aside they are harmless.

**To Test the Freshness of Meats, Game, Etc.**—Thrust a knife blade into center of flesh—remove the blade; your nose to the knife blade will do the rest. Meat is often fresh inside when the outside is not. Your nose can't tell inside—the knife blade can.

**A Good Telescope**—With straps and case is the finest thing for camp and field use. (I never could see why field glasses are preferred.) A good telescope is far better. *(See Telescopes.)*

**For Washing Flannels and Woolens**—Don't wring out, hang them up dripping wet and they won't wrinkle up or shrink.

**To Keep Fresh Cranberries**—Cranberries will keep fresh for weeks if placed in water in a cool place.

**To Keep Fresh Meats, Game, Etc.**—*(See also Smoked Meats, etc.)* By hanging in old sack, sack opening downward; secure with cord, tied to legs of game; then take a few branches of leaves and cover; the rustle of these leaves will help keep the flies away and the meat cool. Fasten the bottom opening with slivers of wood, so you can get at meat without trouble.

**Do Your Part**—Let each man elect to perform certain duties in camp; one to gather wood and carry water, one to cook, one to clean, etc.

**Biscuit Cutter and Rolling Pin**—The tin baking powder can cover makes an excellent biscuit cutter and any bottle a good rolling pin—even an unopened can.

**To Cool Water**—Any old well-soaked cloths, wrapped around outside of bottle or bucket will, if hung in the shade, help cool contents. Remove the cork. *(See Water Cooling Canteens.)*

**A Good Waterproof Oil for Boots and Shoes**—Lay on hot mixture, one part rosin, two parts beeswax, three parts tallow. Soft and waterproof.

**Water and Fireproof for Tents, Canvas, Etc.**—Equal parts of alum and sugar-of-lead, quart or more of each to several buckets of tepid water, soak well, turning often, then spread out to dry. Both rain and fireproof.

**To Waterproof Woolen Clothing**—"Lanolin" (pure sheep wool fat) applied to wool clothing renders it impervious to water. Can be purchased at any drugstore.

**A Tent Closet**—A wire stretched across top of tent poles

makes a good receptacle for clothing at night. *(See also Tent Clothing Hanger.)*

**A Good Camp Bed for Tents, or Tent Carpet**—Take fine ends of any branch clippings, and plenty of them. Commence at head of tent, lay rows of them butts to the rear, in successive layers. If this is done right and carefully and ends locked with a log rolled on so as to hold end in place, an extremely soft bed is the result. Over this spread your tent floor cloth and stake down (or use camp combination).

**If Thirsty and Can't Find Water**—Place a pebble or button in the mouth and keep it there; it will surprise you with the result, and relieve that dryness entirely—try it.

**No Loaded Firearms in Tent**—Don't have loaded firearms in tent; a simple fall of rifle or gun may have serious results; make this a rule.

**Distress Signal**—It is generally understood (or ought to be) that three shots in succession, another shot a minute or so afterward, is a signal of distress.

## LOST IN CAMP

**When you find you have lost your way, don't lose your head**—keep cool; try and not let your brains get into your feet. By this, we mean don't run around and make things worse and play yourself out. First: Sit down and think; cool off, then climb a tree or hill, and endeavor to locate some familiar object you passed, so as to retrace your steps. If it gets dark, build a rousing campfire. Ten to one you will be missed from camp, and your comrades will soon be searching for you, and your fire will be seen by them. (If you have been wise, read your manual and see cooking, etc., without utensils, fire without matches, camp shelter, and the human compass, etc.) Give distress signals, but don't waste all your ammunition thus. It's ten to one morning and a clear head, after a comfortable night (if you make it so), will reveal to you the fact that your camp is much closer to you than you imagined.

I have seen good men lost within rifle shot of camp. A cool head can accomplish much—a rattled one, nothing.

To locate position—note the limbs and bark of trees—the north side of trees can be noted by the thickness and general roughness. Moss most generally is to be found near the roots on the north side. Note also—limbs or longer branches, which generally are to be found longer on south side of trees, while the branches exposed to the north most generally are knotty, twisted, and drooped. In the forest the tops of pine trees dip or trend to the north; also: If you find water, follow it; it generally leads somewhere—where civilization exists. The tendency of people lost is to travel in a circle uselessly; by all means, keep cool and deliberate. Blaze your way by leaving marks on trees to indicate the direction you have taken; read up on this manual, which should be always kept in your pocket when in camp or out; it's made the right size to carry there. A cool head and a stout heart, and lost in camp is really a comedy—not the tragedy—some people make it. This is the time a compass is invaluable.

—"Buzzacott"

**To Make a Fire Without Matches**—Things sometimes invaluable: Such simple facts as these have saved a life many a time. Take a dry handkerchief or cotton lining off your coat, scrape out a very fine lint, a few handfuls, by using the crystal of your watch, compass or spectacle, a sun glass can be made that will ignite the lint, which can be blown to fire.

**Another Way**—Sprinkle powder of cartridge as a fuse to the cotton lint, and with the cartridge percussion cap you can easily ignite the lint, dry moss, leaves, etc.

**Still Another Way**—Take scrapings of very fine pine wood, find a piece of quartz or hard ragged rock, by using your knife as a steel. If you haven't these things, use two pieces of rough, jagged stone and by striking them together sharply in slanting blows you can ignite the lint scrapings. (These are times when a waterproof matchbox and matches are worth their weight in gold.)

**To Dry Inside of Wet Boots, Shoes, Etc.**—The last thing at night take a few handfuls of clean, dry pebbles, heat them in frying pan, kettle, or campfire until very hot, place them in the boots or shoes; they will dry them out thoroughly in a few hours, shake once in a while.

**A Tent Fly**—Makes a capital shelter and shade for your camp cooking and dining purposes. In an emergency it will also serve as a large shelter tent or a large tarpaulin by which you can keep your rations dry, and as an additional shelter to the tent proper when desired. By all means we advise an extra tent fly to be taken along when in camp.

**A Good Compass**—Always carry a good compass to camp. *(See Waterproof Safety Compass.)* It's the kind you need never quarrel with, and if you do, the compass is dead right and you are positively wrong.

**To Make a Good Camp Lantern**—From any ordinary clear glass bottle, if the bottle is long necked. Heat a piece of wire red hot, and wrap it around the part below the neck, the wide part, submerge the neck into a bucket of water, and it will cut the part surrounded by the hot wire as smooth and clean as if cut to order. Now wire a bail or handle to carry it by, with a loop over the bottom, fill one-quarter full with moist dirt or sand, forming a hole therein with a round stick, insert your piece of candle in this hole, cover with a piece of old tin can top (perforated with holes) and you have a good outside camp lantern. A small coil of wire is always a handy thing in camp. *(See camp outfit; it's included therein.)* Common sheet glass can be cut with scissors if held flat under the water while cutting it—try it.

**Don't Sit or Lay on the Bare Ground**—Military statistics have proven beyond question that one-half of the sickness incident to camp and field life is due to neglect of this important caution. Better sit on your hat, anything except the bare ground; even the Indian avoids this, he squats, as he knows it is harmful to even him. The United States government now issues camp cots or beds to the United States troops in camp whenever possible, over 200,000 cots being issued to the United States troops (Gold Medal Brand). By all means avoid sitting or sleeping on the ground, is a golden rule in camp, even though it feels dry.

**Limit of Man's Pack**—Don't forget, 40 pounds is the limit of a man's pack; more is making a pack mule of him.

**Prevent Sickness**—Keep the bowels open, head cool, feet dry and there will be little, if any, sickness in camp.

**Hunter's, Trapper's, and Fisherman's Secrets** for the capture of small game or fish. Take *Cocculus Indicus* (the highly poisonous berry also known as "Levant Nut"), pulverize it, and mix with dough, scatter a few handfuls. In still water where fish frequent, they will seize it voraciously and will immediately become intoxicated and turn belly-up on the water, when they can be gathered in. Now place them in a bucket of water and they will soon revive and be as lively and healthy as ever; this does not injure the fish or the flesh in the slightest way, and is positively harmless. Those you do not wish to use turn loose again; they will soon be all right, as the effects are only temporary and intoxicating only.

**Oil of Rhodium**—A few drops on your bait when fishing with a hook, and fish will never refuse to bite. Add a little of this to bait on small game traps, or oil of amber and oil of rhodium mixed (equal parts) or beaver oil, and the odor will attract them from afar; their scent of this is remarkable and they will risk anything to secure it.

These are reliable secrets of most noted trappers, and the above has been the Chinese secret of catching fish for centuries.

**Birdlime**—As it is sometimes desired to capture, unharmed, for mounting or taxidermists' collections, certain birds, the following receipt will make an excellent sticky birdlime: Common linseed oil or varnish boiled down slowly until a very thick mass; place on limbs or branches where they frequent, or near their nests. I have often used this spread on papers to rid a tent of flies, or I used molasses and flour mixed to a consistency of thick cream and put in a tin plate.

**To Peel Onions**—Dip in water when peeling; they won't make your eyes water.

## VARIOUS CAMPING ADVICE

**Always camp** on a site free from chances of overflow from sudden rains or rise of neighboring creeks and streams. Burn off a clear space if heavy growths of dry grass, brush, etc., prevails; do this carefully lest it get the best of you and a prairie or forest fire result.

Never leave camp without putting out the fire; if no water is at hand use dirt or earth and smother it.

**For Midwinter Work,** a silk and worsted skullcap should be carried along, and for winter work, in high northern altitudes, a thick knitted woolen cap, large enough to come well down over the ears and neck, is desirable; but never wear a fur hat hunting if you value your hair or your health. If you do, your head will get hot when you are walking, the perspiration will run down your neck, you will take off your cap to get relief, and will get a cold in your head that will last you a month.

**About Moccasins**—When a man whose feet have been cased up in tight-fitting leather boots or shoes, and unnatural and ungraceful heels on them all his life, gets out into the woods, and puts on a pair of moccasins for the first time, he feels like the schoolboy who has been shut up within brick walls for six months, with his books, and is turned out on his uncle's farm for his summer vacation; he feels like a racehorse that has been stabled through a long winter, and in the spring is turned out in a field of green clover; he feels like a bird dog that has been housed up in his city kennel all summer, and, in the cool, bright autumn days, is turned loose in the country among the quails or prairie chickens. When a man, I say, whose feet have been pinched and whose corns have been cultivated with leather boots or shoes for years, gets out and gets his first pair of moccasins on, he wants to run, leap, sing, dance, shout, whistle—he wants to do anything that will give vent to his joyous feelings. He would shake hands then with his worst enemy, if he were there, and slap him on the back; he would buy his wife a sealskin sack; he would hug his grandmother.

In ordering them for tender feet specify that double soles be provided, and see that they are made of elk or moose skin, the legs of which should extend half way to the knee, so as to serve as leggings as well. There are only two or three good makers of these things in the country, so look out.

—"Buzzacott"

**To Keep Ants Away from Ration Box**—Nail to the four corners of box small legs or wooden uprights. Place these uprights or legs in center of saucers or old tin cans, partly filled with water or oil; ants cannot get to the box.

**To Find the North Star**—Look for the Big Dipper; the two stars farthest from the handle are the pointers and the big star in line with them is the North Star.

**Don't Use Old Camping Ground**—Rather choose a new location in the immediate vicinity. Pitch your tent so that it will be protected in cold weather from prevailing winds, sheltered by some natural shelter, rising ground, bank, clump of trees, bushes, etc.

**Trees Poor in Fat** are more apt to be struck by lightning than fat trees (the same rule applies in strong winds as branches break). Poor trees are such as poplars, willows, cottonwood, catalpa, locust, etc. Fat trees are bass, birch, butternut, oak, maple, beech, chestnut, etc., etc.

**Good Eating When Camping**—Pick up or cut a bucketful of the tender leaves of dandelion roots, cut off all portions of the roots, keeping only the tender leaves. Wash them in several waters and strain each time so as to get them thoroughly cleansed. Put them in a cook pot and cover with boiling water and a tablespoonful of salt. Boil for five minutes, then strain them well; add fresh boiling water, boil for another five minutes, and you have splendid greens (far better than spinach). A bucketful of the uncooked greens will make, when boiled, a good meal for four to six persons (they are simply delicious), but must be boiled as stated in two waters; season before serving with pepper and salt to taste. If a pound of bacon cut in very small tiny dicelike pieces is added to them when boiling, it will make a complete meal—when cold they are elegant fried and served with fried sliced bacon. Always be sure to wash them thoroughly in plenty of water before boiling them. The liquor they are boiled in is good spring blood medicine also.

**Hang Up Birds and Game**—Birds by the head, game by the tail.

**Pick up Birds**—From the water by their heads, shake them, and they will come out of the water dry; to pick them up by the wing or leg is to lift up water with them and make them soaking wet and heavy. *See our copious Hunting and Shooting notes below, as well as the complete instructions for shooting skeet in* A Man's Life: The Complete Instructions.

**A Common Dutch Oven,** with cover, is one of the best single all-round camping utensils made; in it one can fry, boil, stew, broil, roast, or bake. Never use a soldered utensil over a campfire if you can help it.

**To Put Out Prairie Fires**—If coming toward you and serious, fire a streak between yourself and the fire and place yourself and outfit on the burnt portion. If a small fire in camp or about it, whip or beat it out with wet canvas or a wet gunnysack, green branch of a tree shovel, canvas coat, etc.

**For a Good Sanitary Rule in Camp**—Read Deuteronomy, Chapter 23—10th to 13th verse, and follow the invaluable hint. Take a Bible along; it's a good instructor on camping.

---

### To Splice a Rope

Every farmer and every outdoorsman ought to be able to splice a rope, make a rope halter, and tie all the useful knots known to the sailor. To splice a rope is a simple matter, but to teach the art on paper is quite another thing. However, by carefully following the directions and studying the cuts anyone may learn this useful accomplishment.

Figures 74, 75 and 76 illustrate the beginning of what is known as the short splices. To make it, first untwist the two ends to be spliced for about a foot (more or less according to the size of the rope), and put them together as shown in Fig. 74. Begin splicing by placing the strand A around D, as shown in Fig. 75. Turn the rope toward you and put C around E in the same manner; then B around F. Next turn the rope around; or, in other words, place yourself on the other side of it and

---

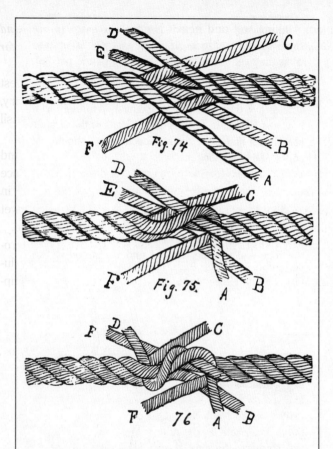

Fig. 74

Fig. 75.

76

put the end D around strand A, as in Fig. 76. Then put F around B in the same manner; then E around C. Now pull all the ends tight and go through the same process again—always twisting the same strands together so that the spliced parts of the rope will consist of three strands, the same as any other part. After proceeding for a few inches cut out a few threads from each strand every time it is put around its mate; in this way the splices will be made to gradually taper toward the ends.

*continued*

In splicing new rope it is often necessary to use some sort of tool to separate the strands. Sailors use what they call a marlinspike (a sort of rude needle), but a short piece of hardwood sharpened at one end answers very well. It is pushed through between the strands and the end of the strand pushed through with it or just behind it. In the cuts the ends of the strands are made short for convenience; they should, of course, be much longer.

## Rope Halter

To make a rope halter take 14 feet of half-inch rope, and about 4 feet from one end form a loop by doubling the rope and passing the end under a strand in two places about 2 inches apart.

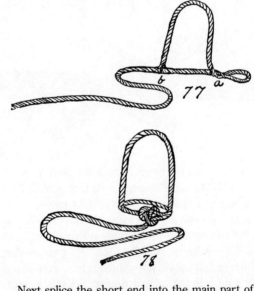

Next splice the short end into the main part of the rope at B. Finish the halter by passing the long end through the loop and tying as in Fig. 78. The end of the rope should be wound with a piece of binding twine, and the ends of the twine, instead of being knotted, should be spliced into the rope so that they will never come out.

### Knots Useful in Handling Livestock and Pack Animals

The bowline knot is one which everyone should know how to tie. It never slips nor comes loose of itself, and no matter how much strain is put upon it, it never becomes jammed so that it cannot be easily untied. For fastening the hay-fork rope to the whiffletrees or tying a rope around a calf's neck this knot cannot be excelled. Fig. 79 shows how it is made.

In these days of dehorned cattle it is often necessary

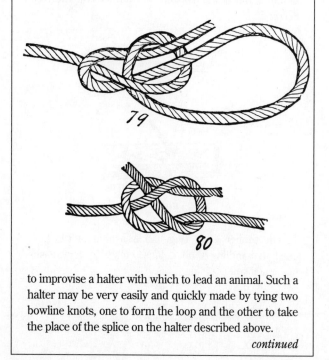

to improvise a halter with which to lead an animal. Such a halter may be very easily and quickly made by tying two bowline knots, one to form the loop and the other to take the place of the splice on the halter described above.

*continued*

The weaver's knot (shown in Fig. 80), bears a close relationship to the bowline knot, as a careful study of both knots will show. It is used by weavers in tying the ends of warp together. Like the bowline knot, it will never slip; neither will it jam so as to be hard to untie. It is a good knot to use in tying two straps together.

Fig. 81 shows a way of attaching a rope to any smooth or slippery object which is to be pulled endwise; for instance a pump, a pipe of any kind, or a round log. The cut shows so plainly how to attach the rope that a description is hardly needed. A slip knot is made and the rope is wrapped several times around the object. When the end is pulled upon, the rope hugs the object so tightly that slipping is impossible. The stronger the power applied, the tighter will the rope become.

FIG. 81.

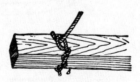

FIG. 82.

The timber hitch (Fig. 82) is a kind of slip knot used in handling timber, logs, etc. It is very easily made and will not jam.

## The Long Splice

The accompanying cut shows how to make what sailors call the "long splice" in a rope.

The length of a long splice should be about 100 diameters of the rope for large rope and 80 diameters for small rope.

Suppose we have a splice to make a ¾-inch hay-fork rope. Unravel each rope for a distance of about three feet, and set them together in such a way that each of the unravelled strands shall be between two strands of the opposite rope. Now twist adjacent strands together in pairs as in Fig. 1. This twisting is done to avoid confusion and tangling and is not part of the splicing proper. In the cut one rope is represented as black, and the other white to make the operation more plain, and the strands of the black rope are numbered 1, 2, and 3, and those of the white rope are lettered A, B, and C. After twisting B and 2 and C and 3 together in pairs, proceed with the splicing by unlaying strand 1 a turn or two and laying strand A in its place; continue this process for a distance of about 2½ feet and leave as in Fig. 2. These figures are shortened to save space and the strands are shown much shorter than they would be in the real rope. Next unlay C and lay 3 in its place the same distance as in the case of A and 1. Each pair of strands is now to be subjected to the following treatment: For convenience we will take strands 3 and C. Unlay each of these strands and slip in halves as in Fig. 4; then lay one half of each strand back where the whole strand came from and tie as in Fig. 5. Be very careful to tie *exactly* as shown in the figure, that is, have C pass around 3 so that when pulled down tight they will form a smooth strand and not be lumpy as they are sure to be if put around each other the wrong way.

*continued*

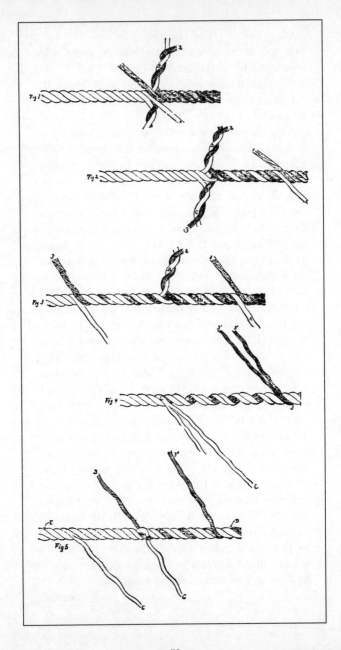

Continue to tuck C around 3 till just past the place where strand 3 was split (point D in the cut), then in the same manner tuck 3 around C till the point E is reached. Now cut off the ends of the half strands about a quarter of an inch from the rope. After treating the other two pairs of strands in the same manner, the splice will be complete.

Two or three precautions are necessary to observe in order to make a smooth splice. Be sure that the strands are set together properly at the start so that each strand goes in between two strands from the opposite rope. In replacing one strand with another, be sure to give the same amount of twist as it had in the original rope.

After tying the half strands and beginning to tuck one around the other, pull on both to draw up tight, otherwise a bunchy, loose place will be left.

—Rolfe Cobleigh

# WHAT TO THINK ABOUT WHEN ALONE IN THE WOODS

## Curious Properties of Some Figures

To multiply by 2 is the same to multiply by 10 and divide by 5.

Any number of figures you may wish to multiply by 5 will give the same result if divided by 2—a much quicker operation than the former; but you must remember to annex a cipher to the answer where there is no remainder, and where there is a remainder, annex a 5 to the answer. Thus, multiply 464 by 5, the answer will be 2,320; divide the same number by 2, and you have 232, and as there is no remainder, you add a cipher. Now, take 357 and multiply by 5—the answer is

1,785. On dividing 357 by 2, there is 178, and a remainder; you therefore place 5 at the right of the line, and the result is again 1,785.

There is something more curious in the properties of the number 9. Any number multiplied by 9 produces a sum of figures which, added together, continually make 9. For example, all the first multiples of 9, as 18, 27 , 36, 45, 54, 63, 72, 81, sum up 9 each. Each of them multiplied by any number whatever produces a similar result; as 8 times 81 are 648, these added together make 18, 1 and 8 are 9. Multiply 648 by itself, the product is 419,904—the sum of these digits is 27, 2 and 7 are 9. The rule is invariable.

Take any number whatever and multiply it by 9; or any multiple of 9, and the sum will consist of figures which, added together, continually number 9. As $17 \times 18 = 306$, 6 and 3 are 9; $117 \times 27 = 3,159$, the figures sum up to 18, 8 and 1 are 9; $4,591 \times 72 = 330,552$, the figures sum up to 18, 8 and 1 are 9. Again, $87,363 \times 54 = 4,717,422$; added together, the product is 27, or 2 and 7 are 9, and so always.

## What to Read from the Bible When Alone in the Woods

*If you are down with the blues,* read the twenty-seventh Psalm.

*If there is a chilly sensation about the heart,* read the third chapter of Revelation.

*If you don't know where to look for the month's rent,* read the thirty-seventh Psalm.

*If you feel lonesome and unprotected,* read the ninety-first Psalm.

*If you find yourself losing confidence in men,* read the thirteenth chapter of First Corinthians.

*If the people pelt you with hard words,* read the fifteenth chapter of John.

*If you are all out of sorts,* read the twelfth chapter of Hebrews.

—"Buzzacott"

## What to Read When Alone in the Woods Because You Are Perplexed by Life's Vicissitudes

*If you have been driven to the woods because you have been confused by women,* read *The Modern Man's Guide to Modern Women,* available only from our Office.

*If you are in the woods because of a peculiar grooming problem,* read the exhaustive entries on the subject in *A Man's Life: The Complete Instructions.*

*If you have found yourself in the woods with a woman and wish to find a means of relating to her feelings,* read *The Modern Woman's Guide to Life,* compiled by three women, also available from our Office.

*If you are camped in the woods because you don't think you can make it in the big city,* read our advice on urban tenting in *A Man's Life: The Complete Instructions.*

*If you are alone in the woods with nothing but a tenderloin of beef and a blowtorch,* consult the explicit culinary instructions found in *The Modern Man's Guide to Life.*

## THE CAMP DOCTOR

*See also our excellent Camp Medicine Case and Medicine therein and the excellent chapter on Health in* A Man's Life: The Complete Instructions.

Keep the bowels open, the head cool, the feet dry and there will little, if any, sickness in camp.

As a rule there is very little need for the use of drugs but as it is well to be prepared for any emergency the few simple rules herein will not prove amiss. Generally speaking we can cure here almost anything in a most unique way. Especially headaches.

Should, however, any very serious accidents happen we advise the preliminary precautions and rules of the manual and in the meantime send one of the party to the nearest settlement for a physician or transport the patient there at once.

How a capital stretcher can be improvised: See "Camp-bed."

**Constipation**—Give doses compound cathartic pills, eat freely of preserves; drink often.

**Diarrhoea**—Apply warm bandages to stomach; fire brown a little flour to which two teaspoonfuls of vinegar and one teaspoonful of salt is added; mix and drink. This is a cure, nine cases out of ten. A tablespoonful of warm vinegar and teaspoonful of salt will cure most severe cases. Don't eat fruit. A hot drink of ginger tea is good. Repeat every few hours the above.

**Cuts and Wounds**—In bleeding from wounds or recent amputations press the finger or hand over the bleeding point, pressing on the main artery supplying the blood to the wound. If this is not possible, apply a bandage as tightly as possible above the wound. By tying a handkerchief loosely around the limb, thrusting a short stick through it and twisting it tightly an excellent tourniquet may be improvised.

The blood from an artery which has been severed is a bright red, and comes in spurts with each beat of the heart. The color of the blood from an ordinary cut is of a dark purplish shade, and flows in a steady stream. All cuts should be washed out with warm water, to which one or two drops of carbolic acid has been added. The edges of the wound should then be brought together and held in position by strips of plaster, then bound up tightly with clean bandages.

**Cramps and Chills**—Mix pepper and ginger in very hot water and drink. Give dose of cramp tablets.

*A hot stone* makes a good foot warmer.

**Fevers**—Give doses of quinine tablets; loosen bowels if necessary; keep dry and warm.

**Fishhook**—If a fish hook gets caught in the flesh, push it on through and when the end sticks out, break off the hook and pull it out the other way. Put tincture of iodine on the wound and bandage.

**Sore Throat**—Fat bacon or pork tied on with a dry stocking; keep on until soreness is gone, then remove fat and keep covering it a day longer. Tincture of iron diluted; swab the throat.

**Burns**—Use common baking soda, dry flour, camp fat or oil, or mix as a paste.

**Scalds**—Relieve instantly with common baking soda and soaking wet rags—dredge the soda on thick and wrap wet clothes thereon. To dredge with flour is good also.

**Colds**—Put on warm, dry clothing. Drink freely of hot ginger tea; cover well at night; give dose of quinine every six hours.

**Toothache**—Warm vinegar and salt. Hold in mouth around tooth until pain ceases, or plug cavity with cotton mixed with pepper and ginger.

**Headache**—Among soldiers and outdoorsmen, headache is usually due to intestinal indigestion, combined with a congestion of the stomach. Take a tablespoonful of Worcestershire sauce or five drops of Tabasco sauce in a tumbler of hot water as a drink and put a small piece of soap up into the bowel to cause a movement.

**Poultices**—Common soap and sugar, mixed; stale or fresh bread, mustard and flour, equal parts mixed with vinegar or water.

**Ivy Poison**—Relieved with solution of baking soda and water; use freely as cooling wash. Keep the bowels open.

**Poisoning**—Give strong emetic of warm water, mustard, and salt. Cause vomiting by swallowing small piece of soap, tobacco, etc., if by no other means.

**Poisons**—In all cases of poisoning there should be no avoidable delay in summoning a physician. The most important thing is that the stomach should be emptied at once. If the patient is able to swallow this may be accomplished by emetics, such as mustard and water, a teaspoonful of mustard to a glass of water, salt and water, powdered ipecac, and copious draughts of lukewarm water. Vomiting may also be induced by tickling the back of the throat with a feather. When the patient begins to vomit, care should be taken to support the head in order that the vomited matter may be ejected at once, and not swallowed again or drawn into the windpipe.

**Poisonous Snake Bites**—Suck the wound instantly and thoroughly (it is perfectly safe if no sores are in the mouth); sear with red-hot iron; cut out wound if necessary and with red-hot knife burn it out so as to destroy entire surface. It requires nerve but a life depends on it. Act at once. Keep cool. Ammonia is one of the best antidotes for snake bites known. Apply externally.

**Insect Bites, Wasps, Etc.**—Common mud is excellent; use plenty of it. Crushed pennyroyal weed keeps mosquitoes away.

**Drowning**—A drowning man may just as likely drown his would-be rescuer unless precautions are observed.

*Rescuing.* Approach the drowning man from behind, seizing him by the coat collar, or a woman by the back hair, and tow at arm's length to boat or shore. Do not let him cling around your neck or arms to endanger you. Duck him until unconscious if necessary to break a dangerous hold upon you; but do not strike to stun him.

A drowning man *does not* come to the top three times before giving up.

*Reviving.* When a person is apparently drowned he is unconscious and not breathing because his lungs are full of water and his skin is blue and cold because no air is getting into his blood to redden it and warm it; *remember* the heart does not stop until some time after their breathing stops. If we can get air into the blood and start breathing again before the heart stops we can save the patient's life. If we cannot get the breath started in time the heart stops and the patient is then dead.

Our problem then is this:

1. To get the water out of the lungs.
2. To get the air into the lungs and start the man breathing before the heart stops.

Emptying the lungs is precisely similar to emptying a bottle.

The lungs are the bottle, the windpipe is the neck of the bottle and the cork of the bottle may be the tongue turned back in the throat or mud and leaves from bottom of the pool and bloody froth in the nostrils. We therefore—

1. Pull out the cork. *Remove mud, mucus, etc., and pull the tongue forward.*

2. Turn the bottleneck down to pour out the contents. *Place the patient's head lower than his chest so the water will run out.*

*Artificial respiration.* Then lay the patient on a blanket, if possible, and on his stomach, arms extended from his body beyond his head, face turned to one side so that the mouth and nose do not touch the ground. This position causes the tongue to fall forward of its own weight and so prevents it from falling back into the air passages. Turning the head to one side prevents the face coming into contact with mud or water during the operation.

Kneel and straddle the patient's hips, facing his head.

Roll up or rip off the clothing so as to get at the bare back.

Locate the lowest rib, and with your thumbs extending in about the same direction as your fingers, place your spread hands so that your little finger curls over the lowest rib. *Be sure to get the hands well away from the backbone*—the nearer the ends of the ribs the hands are placed without sliding off, the better it is.

Then with your arms *held straight,* press down SLOWLY AND STEADILY on the ribs, bringing the weight of your body straight from your shoulders. *Do not bend your elbows and shove in from the side.*

Release the pressure suddenly, removing the hands from the body entirely, and thus allowing the chest to fill with air.

Wait a couple of seconds, so as to give the air time to get into the blood. This is most important.

Repeat the pressure and continue doing so, slowly and steadily, pressing down at the rate of ordinary breathing. That is to say, pressure and release of pressure (one complete respiration) should occupy about five seconds. Guide yourself by your own deep, regular breathing, or by counting.

Keep up for at least one hour the effort to revive the patient; and much longer if there is any sign of revival by way of speaking, breathing, coughing, sneezing, or gurgling sounds.

Do not stop working at the first signs of life, but keep it up until the patient is breathing well and is conscious. If you stop too soon he may stop breathing and die.

Persons have been revived after two hours of steady

work, but most cases revive within about thirty minutes.

If you are a heavy man, be careful not to bring too much force on the ribs, as you might break one of them.

In the case of women or thin persons place a roll of clothing under them at the waistline before beginning the pressure.

If you happen to be of light build and the patient is a large, heavy person, you will be able to apply the pressure better by raising your knees from the ground, and supporting yourself entirely on your toes and the heels of your hands, properly placed on the floating ribs the patient.

*Do not attempt to give liquids of any kind to the patient while he is unconscious,* for he cannot swallow them. They will merely run into his windpipe and choke him, and furthermore, it will take up valuable time.

However, after the patient has regained consciousness you may give him hot coffee or hot whiskey, punch, or aromatic spirits of ammonia (a teaspoonful in water).

Then wrap up the patient warmly in hot blankets with hot water bottles, and take him to the nearest hospital or put him to bed and send for a doctor. Why? Because the dirty water in the lungs has damaged the lining and the patient is in danger of lung fever and needs care and nursing.

Aromatic spirits of ammonia may be poured on a handkerchief and held continually within about three inches of the face and nose. If other ammonia preparations are used, they should be diluted or held farther away. Try it on your own nose first.

The above method of artificial respiration is also applicable in cases of electric shock, suffocation by gas, and smoke.

**Earache**—Put a teaspoonful of salt into a quart of water and add six teaspoonfuls of tea. Boil it. As soon as it is cool enough to stand the finger, drip some into the nostrils until it falls into the throat. Clear out the nose and throat by sniffing—*do not blow* the nose—and then gargle with the rest of the remedy as hot as can be taken, holding each mouthful well back in the throat. This will often open up the tubes running from the ears to the throat, and relieve the pressure against the eardrum. In addition, a little hot oil may be dropped into the ear. Repeat the treatment in one-half hour if not successful first time.

*A piece of cotton sprinkled with pepper* and moistened with oil or fat will give almost instant relief. Wash with hot water.

**Insects in Ear**—Use warm oil or fat. Wash well in hot water.

**Mosquito Ointment**—Solution ammonia or camphor or tar soap. Apply bruised pennyroyal.

**Another One**—2 ounces pine tar, 2 ounces castor oil (olive, sweet oil, or melted tallow will do as well), 1 ounce of pennyroyal; simmer slowly over slow fire and cover tightly in 6-ounce bottle.

**Cuts, Bleeding, Etc.**—Wrap with common paper; use mixture of flour and salt. Bind on until it stops bleeding. In extreme cases tie a handkerchief over part nearest the body and with a stick, twist up good and tight, then dress the wound and gently remove.

**Ointment for Bruises, Etc.**—Wash with hot water then anoint with tallow or candle grease.

**Sprains**—Apply cold water application and cloths.

**Sore and Blistered Feet**—Wash in warm water, then bathe well in cold water to which a little baking soda had been added—wipe dry and anoint with tallow from candle or fat. Keep the feet clean; dirty feet and socks make sore ones. Soap well the stockings (using common soap) until the feet harden—this is an excellent method.

**To Quench Thirst**—Don't drink too often, better rinse out the mouth often, taking a swallow or two only. A pebble or button kept in the mouth will help quench that dry and parched tongue.

**Inflamed Eyes**—Bind on hot tea leaves or raw fresh meat. Leave on overnight. Wash well in morning with warm water.

**Keep Head Cool**—By placing wet green leaves inside of hat.

**Convulsions**—Give hot baths at once; rub well the lower parts of the body to stimulate; keep water as hot as possible without scalding, then dry and wrap up very warm.

**Struck by Lightning**—Handle the body gently. Loosen any clothing. Carry the body face downward, with the head slightly raised. No time should be lost in following out the instruction given below, which should be continued for hours without ceasing, or until a physician, who should be summoned immediately, shall arrive. The body should be stripped of all clothing, rubbed dry, and placed in bed in a warm place. Warmth should be supplied to the body by hot water bottles or some other appliance. Cleanse the mouth of any dirt or mucus that may be in it, and draw the tongue forward with a handkerchief, holding it with the finger and thumb. This is most important, as it opens the windpipe, and should not be neglected. The patient should be placed upon his back, with head and shoulders slightly elevated. The operator standing behind his head should grasp the arms just above the elbow and draw them steadily and gently upward until they meet above the head, then bring them down to the side of the chest slowly and persistently at the rate of twenty times to the minute. These movements imitate expiration and respiration. The trunk and limbs should be rubbed when breathing commences, and a stimulant or warm drink given.

**Bathing**—Be careful in strange places. Don't dive; weeds may be at bottom or sharp rocks. Water that looks inviting often is full of treacherous, slimy weeds in which once caught it is almost impossible to get free. Look out for deep unseen mud holes. Better splash water over body than to take big risks.

**Choking**—If possible force water down the throat or push down substance with spoon handle. Hearty slapping on the back is also effective. Getting on all-fours will help matters.

**Freezing**—At all hazards keep awake. Take a stick and beat each other unmercifully; to restore circulation to frozen limbs rub with snow; when roused again don't stop or fall asleep—it is certain death. Remember this and rouse yourself.

**Snow or Sun Blindness**—Smear the nose and face about the eyes with charcoal.

Use raw onions for insect bites and stings.

**About Canned Goods**—These are OK for any permanent camp, but if you pack your outfits and transportation is limited don't carry too much canned stuff, especially those of the delusive kind that are two-thirds water. The chances are you'll find better water where you are going to camp, and save the freight.

Fruits, etc., are dried or evaporated in such excellent style nowadays that there is little need of carrying them about, put up or preserve in containers.

Have your provisions put up in canvas bags with strings to secure them (ration bags); don't risk paper ones. If you do you are apt to find things sadly mixed at some stage of the trip.

**In Wintertime**—If freezing cold—campers, hunters, etc., should never remove snow from ground on which they pitch camp, better heap up more snow—(inside and outside) to dig down to the ground would be to dig up cold and discomfort—snow is a warm and soft bed—compared to hard frozen ground. Arctic explorers always choose the protection of the biggest snow banks they can find; even animals, birds, etc., burrow holes into them to secure warmth.

**For Frozen Fingers, Nose, Ears, Etc.**—Never rub with snow. The one who recommends rubbing such tender members with snow is a fool. Instead, clasp the frozen member with the warm hand firmly so as the warmth of the hand will thaw it out; to rub such a member already frozen with snow is to break the skin and do much harm and cause much pain. Common sense tells a man you can't thaw ice by making it colder. A good way (if it can be done) is to dip the member into cold water, then pour in warm water gradually until of a good blood heat.

Returning pinkness is a sign of thawing; if the parts turn a dark color, see a surgeon at once, for it means gangrene (death of the flesh).

When thawed out, apply plenty of oil, tallow, or Vaseline.

If gangrene has set in and no doctor is available, then treat as a burn.

By all means keep away from extreme heat. To toast frostbitten fingers or toes before a fire is liable to result in chilblains.

## Reliable Weather Signs
*Pale yellow sky at Sunset* indicates wet weather
*Red Sunrise* indicates Rain and Wind
"Red at night, Camper's delight;
Red in Morning, Camper's warning."
"Rain before seven, quits before eleven."

Rain with East Wind is lengthy

Red Eastern Sky at sunset means bad weather to come

Sudden Rain, short duration

Slow rain lasts long

When beetles fly expect a fine to-morrow

Busy spiders mean fine weather

Flies bite harder on approaching storms

When dogs sniff the air frequently look for a change in the
weather

Morning rains make clear afternoons

Birds flying high indicate good weather

Birds and animals travel away from water in the morning,
toward water at night

Hiding spiders or breaking webs indicate storms

Heavy dew means dry weather to follow

When birds ruffle or pick their feathers, huddle together,
look out for changes in the weather

Low clouds swiftly moving indicate coolness and rain

Gray morning sky means good weather

Soft-looking clouds mean fine weather to come, moderate
winds

Hard-edged clouds, light winds

Rolled or ragged clouds heavy winds

A strip of seaweed, in tent or house, in fine weather, keeps dry
and dusty-like; in coming rains it gets wet, damp and sticky

*See also our Weather Table, below, and our Forecasting
information.*

**To Tell the Points of the Compass with a Watch**—When
the sun is to be seen (for men do even get lost in sunlight),
put down your watch with the hour hand pointing directly
toward the sun—halfway between the hour hand and figure
twelve is south.

**Do not kill more game than you need or can use;** don't be a hog.

**Do not fire** at an object until you are sure it is not a human being.

## WEATHER TABLE: FOR FORETELLING THE WEATHER THROUGHOUT ALL THE LUNATIONS OF EACH YEAR—FOREVER

This table and the accompanying remarks are the results of many years actual observation, the whole being constructed on a due consideration of the attraction of the sun and moon, in their several positions respecting the earth, and will, by simple inspection, show the observer what kind of weather will most probably follow the entrance of the moon into any of its quarters, and that so near the truth, as to be seldom or never found to fail.

### If the New Moon, First Quarter, Full Moon, or Last Quarter, Happens

|  | In Summer | In Winter |
|---|---|---|
| Between midnight and 2 o'clock | Fair | Frost, unless wind southwest |
| " 2 and 4 morning | Cold and showers | Snow and stormy |
| " 4 and 6 | Rain | Rain |
| " 8 and 10 | Wind and rain | Stormy |
| " 10 and 12 | Changeable | Cold rain if wind west, snow if east |
| " 12 and 2 P.M. | Frequent showers | Cold and high wind |
| " 2 and 4 | Very rainy | Snow or rain |
| " 4 and 6 | Changeable | Fair and mild |
| " 6 and 8 | Fair | Fair |
| " 8 and 10 | Fair if wind northwest | Fair & frosty if wind north or northeast |
| " 10 and midnight | Rainy if south, or southwest | Rain or snow if south or southwest |
|  | Fair | Fair and frosty |

## FORECASTING INFORMATION: COMPLETELY ACCURATE METHODS FOR FORECASTING WEATHER IN RURAL AREAS

*For storms*—Storms are most frequent in December, January, and February. In September, there are generally one or two storms. If it blows in the day, it generally hushes towards evening; but if it continue blowing then, it may be expected to continue. The vernal equinoctial gales are stronger than the autumnal.

*Dew*—If the dew lies plentifully on the grass after a fair day, it is a sign of another. If not, and there is no wind, rain must follow. A red evening portends fine weather; but if it spread too far upwards from the horizon in the evening, and especially morning, it foretells wind or rain, or both. When the sky, in rainy weather, is tinged with sea green, the rain will increase. If with deep blue, it will be showery.

*Clouds*—Against much rain, the clouds grow bigger, and increase very fast, especially before thunder. When the clouds are formed like fleeces, but dense in the middle and bright towards the edges, with the sky bright, they are signs of a frost, with hail, snow, or rain. If clouds form high in the air, in thin white tails like locks of wool, they portend wind, and probably rain. When a general cloudiness covers the sky, and small black fragments of clouds fly underneath, they are a sure sign of rain, and probably it will be lasting. Two currents of clouds always portend rain, and, in summer, thunder.

*Heavenly Bodies*—A haziness in the air, which fades the sun's light, and makes the orb appear whitish, or ill-defined—or at night, if the moon and stars grow dim, and a ring encircles the former, rain will follow. If the sun's rays appear like Moses' horns—if while at setting, or shorn of his rays, or goes down into a bank of clouds in the horizon, bad weather is to be expected. If the moon looks pale and dim, we expect rain; if red, wind; and if of her natural color, with a clear sky, fair weather. If the moon is rainy throughout, it will be clear at the change, and perhaps rain returns a few days after. If fair throughout, and rain at the change, the fair weather will probably return on the fourth or fifth day.

*For the Approach of Thunder*—If an east wind blow against a heavy sky from the westward, the wind decreasing in force as the clouds approach.

If the clouds rise and twist in different directions.

If the birds be silent.

If cattle run round and collect together in meadows.

*For Continued Thunder Showers*—If there be showery weather, with sunshine, and increase of heat in the spring, a thunderstorm may be expected every day, or at least every other day.

*Signs of the Abatement of Thunder Showers*—If the air be very dry, with clear, yet cooler weather, or in one or two following days, the atmosphere be heavy, with a little damp falling.

With a north wind it seldom thunders; but with a south and southwest wind, often.

# Angling

## Average Size and Strength of Various Fishing Lines (Braided, Linen, and Silk)

6 or H

5 or G

4 or F

3 or E

2 or D

1 or C

*Above illustrations are made as near correct as a cut can be made from the almost invisible line.*

**6 or H**—Tests  10  to  12 to 20 lbs.
**5 or G**—Tests  12  to  15 to 25 lbs.
**4 or F**—Tests  18  to  20 to 30 lbs.
**3 or E**—Tests  22  to  25 to 35 lbs.
**2 or D**—Tests  30  to  35 to 40 lbs.
**1 or C**—Tests  40  to  45 to 50 lbs.

**Raw Silk Lines**—Are made from raw silk containing the natural gum of the silkworm.

**Finished Silk Lines**—Have all the natural gum boiled out, reducing the size of the line, *yet still preserving its full original strength.* For instance, a size 5 finished silk line is slightly smaller than a No. 5 raw silk, yet fully as strong.

(This treatment adds to its cost.)

**Oiled Silk Lines**—A raw silk line that has been soaked in oil, rendering it *practically waterproof* and as strong as the raw or finished silk line.

**Enameled Silk Line**—A line that has been treated with a preparation giving it a hard and glossy surface, which becomes flexible when used in water.

**Tested Strength**—The tested strength given above is for wet lines (as in use); when dry a line will test from 20 to 25 percent more (unless thoroughly waterproof), so bear that in mind.

Test, of course, varies according to whether lines are of first quality or not.

### Approximate Weight of Trout from Actual Measurements

| | | |
|---|---|---|
| 8-inch Trout | weighs | 4 ounces. |
| 9-inch Trout | weighs | 5 ounces. |
| 10-inch Trout | weighs | 7 ounces. |
| 11-inch Trout | weighs | 9 ounces. |
| 12-inch Trout | weighs | 1 pound. |
| 15-inch Trout | weighs | 1½ pounds. |
| 18-inch Trout | weighs | 2½ pounds. |
| 24-inch Trout | weighs | 4–6 pounds. |

## HOW TO MAKE A FISHING ROD

The pleasures of outdoor life are most keenly enjoyed by those sportsmen who are familiar with all the little tricks—the "ins and outs"—of the open. It is the active participation in any chosen sport that makes the sport well worthwhile, for the enjoyment gleaned from little journeys to forest and stream largely rests with the man's own knowledge of his sport. Not all of the fun of fishing lies in the catching of the fish, since the satisfaction that comes through handling a well-balanced rod and tackle must be reckoned the chief contributor to the outing. In other words, the pleasures of fishing do not depend so much upon the number of fish caught as the manner in which the person fishes for them. The rod is naturally the first and important consideration in the angler's kit, and it is the purpose of these articles to set forth, at first, a few hints that my own long experience leads me to think may be of some assistance to those anglers who enjoy making and repairing their own rods and tackle, to be followed, later, by some suggestions on the art of angling generally. The hints given are merely my own methods, and while they may not be the best way of accomplishing the desired end, a good fishing rod may be constructed. Like the majority of amateurs, I have achieved the desired results with a few common tools, namely, a saw, plane, jackknife, file, and sandpaper. These simple tools are really all that is needed to turn out a serviceable and well-finished rod of excellent action.

## Kind of Material

The great elasticity and durability of the split-cane or split-bamboo rod cannot be easily disputed. The handmade split bamboo is unquestionably the best rod for every kind of fishing, but it is also the most expensive and the most difficult material for the amateur to work. In making the first rod or two, the beginner will be better satisfied with the results in making a good solid-wood rod. Of course, glued-up split-bamboo butts, joints, and tip stock may be purchased, and if the angler is determined to have only bamboo, it is advisable to purchase these built-up sections rather than to risk certain failure by attempting to glue the cane. However, there are several good woods particularly well adapted for rod making, and while slightly inferior to the finest bamboo in elasticity and spring, the carefully made solid-wood rod is good enough for any angler and will probably suit the average fisherman as well as any rod that can be purchased.

Bethabara, or washaba, a native wood of British Guinea, makes a fine rod, but it is a heavy wood, very hard, and for this reason is perhaps less desirable than all other woods. With the single exception of snakewood it is the heaviest wood for rod making and is only used for short bait-casting rods. Possessing considerable strength, bethabara can be worked quite slender, and a five-foot casting tip can be safely made of five-ounce weight.

Greenheart, a South American wood, is popular alike with manufacturers and amateur rod makers, and 90 percent of the better class of solid-wood rods are made of this material. It resembles bethabara in color, but is lighter in weight, although it apparently possesses about the same strength and elasticity. In point of fact, there is little, if any, choice between these woods, and providing sound and well-selected wood is used, the merits of a rod made of bethabara or greenheart are more likely to be due to the careful workmanship of the maker than to the variety of the wood used.

Dagame, or dagama, a native of the forests of Cuba, is in many respects the ideal material for rod making, as it has strength and elasticity. This wood is straight-grained and free from knots, which makes it easily worked; it polishes well and is durable. While there is always more or less difficulty about procuring first-class bethabara and greenheart, dagame of good quality is easily obtained.

Lancewood is much used in turning out the cheaper grades of fishing rods, but it is somewhat soft and has a marked tendency to take set under the strain of fishing and warp out of shape. It is less expensive than the other woods, and while it has a straight and even grain, there are numerous small knots present that make this material less satisfactory to work than the other woods. For heavy sea rods, lancewood may serve the purpose fairly well, but for the smaller fishing tools this material is inferior to bethabara, greenheart, and dagame. Other woods are often used, and while a good rod may be frequently made from almost any of them, the three mentioned are held in the highest esteem by the angling fraternity. For the first rod, the amateur will make no mistake in selecting dagame, whether the slender fly rod or the more easily constructed short bait-casting tool is to be made.

## The Necessary Tools

The construction of a thoroughly well-made and nicely balanced rod is more a matter of careful work than outfit, but a few suitable tools will greatly facilitate the labor. A good firm workbench, or table, four feet or more in length, will be needed. A regulation bench vise will come in handy, but one of the small iron vises will do very well. A couple of iron planes, one of medium size for rough planing-up work, and a small four-inch block plane for finishing, will be required. As the cutters of the planes must be kept as sharp as possible to do good work, a small oilstone—preferably one in a wood case with cover to keep out dust—will be needed; a coarse single-cut mill file about sixteen inches long; a few sheets of No. 1 and No. 0 sandpaper; a sheet or two of fine emery cloth; a small thin "back" or other saw, and a steel cabinet scraper.

A caliper of some kind is a necessity, and while the best is a micrometer, Fig. 1, registering to a thousandth part of an inch, as well as indicating 8ths, 16th, 32ds, and 64ths, this tool is somewhat expensive, but a very good caliper may be had in the sliding-arm type, Fig. 2, with the scale graduated

Fig.1      Fig.2      Fig.3

to 64ths and taking work up to two inches in diameter. Cheaper measuring gauges are to be had in plenty, but as the brass and boxwood scales are provided only with coarse graduations, the better quality of mechanics' tools will give better satisfaction.

The set of grooved planes used by the professional rod makers are rather expensive, although they are most convenient for quickly rounding up the rod to the desired diameter. However, the beginner may dispense with the planes by making the tool illustrated in Fig. 3. To make this handy little tool purchase a steel wood scraper, such as cabinetmakers use, and file a series of grooves along the edges with a round file. File at right angles to the steel, finishing up with a finer file to give a sharp cutting edge. The tool thus made is very handy for scraping the rod after it has been roughly rounded with the plane. Its use will be mentioned later on in the description.

### Five-Foot Bait-Casting Rod

The short one-piece bait-casting rod with but one ferrule is the easiest rod to make, and for this reason the beginner will do well to select this popular type for the first attempt. As the total length of the rod is to measure five feet, exclusive of the agate tip, the wood should be one or two inches longer to allow for cutting down to sixty inches.

Having selected a good strip of dagame, ⅝ inch square, run the plane along each side and from both ends. This will

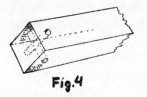

**Fig. 4**

determine the direction in which the grain runs. Drill two holes at the end decided upon for the butt, spacing them about ¼ inch from the end, as shown in Fig. 4. Drive a stout brad in the corner of the bench top and hook the butt end over the nail. By rigging the stick up in this manner it will be securely held, and planing may be done with the grain with greater ease and accuracy than when the end of the stick is butted up against a cleat nailed to the benchtop.

The wood should be planed straight and true from end to end and calipered until it is ½ inch square. It may appear crooked, but this need not trouble one at this stage of the work, since it may be made perfectly straight later on. Overlook any kinks, and do not attempt to straighten the stick by planing more from one side than the other. The chief thing to be done is to fashion a square stick, and when the caliper shows the approximate diameter, draw crosslines at the end to find the center.

The length of the hand grasp should be marked out. If a double grasp is wanted, allow 12 inches from the butt end. This will afford an 11-inch hand grasp after sawing off the end in which the holes were drilled. For a single hand grasp make an allowance of 11 inches. However, the double grasp—with cork above and below the reel seat—is preferred by most anglers because it affords a better grip for the hand when reeling in the line. Mark the hand-grasp distance by running a knife mark around the rod 12 inches from the butt end.

Lay out a diagram showing the full length of the rod by placing a strip of paper—the unprinted back of a strip of wall-paper is just the thing—on the bench and drawing two lines from the diameter of the butt to that of the tip. While the caliber of casting rods differs somewhat, the dimensions given will suit the average angler, and I would advise the beginner to make the rod to these measurements. For the butt, draw a line, exactly ½ inch long, across the paper and from the center of this line run a straight pencil mark at right angles to the tip end, or 60 inches distant, at which point another crossline is drawn, exactly ⅛ inch long, to represent the diameter. Connect the ends of these two crosslines to make a long tapering form. Divide this pattern into eight equal parts, beginning at 12 inches from the butt end, making a crossline at every 6 inches. This layout is shown exaggerated in Fig. 5.

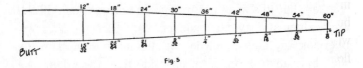

Fig. 5

If it is desired to copy a certain rod, find the diameter at the several 6-inch stations with the caliper and write them down at the corresponding sections of the paper diagram. However, if a splendid all-around casting rod is desired, it is perfectly safe to follow the dimensions given in Fig. 5, which show the manner of dividing the paper pattern into the equal parts and the final diameter of the rod at each 6-inch station, or line.

Procure a small strip of thin brass, or zinc, and file nine slots on one edge to correspond in diameter with the width of the horizontal lines, which indicate the diameter of the rod on the pattern. This piece is shown in Fig. 6.

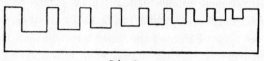

Fig. 6

By making use of the pattern and the brass gauge, the rod may be given the desired taper and the work will proceed more quickly than if the caliper is alone relied upon to repeatedly check up the work.

When a good layout of the work is thus made, the next step is to carefully plane the stick so that it will be evenly tapered in the square. Plane with the grain and from the butt toward the tip end, and make frequent tests with caliper and gauge, noting the diameter every 6 inches. Mark all the thick spots with a pencil, and plane lightly to reduce the wood to the proper diameter. Reduce the stick in this manner until all sides have an even taper from the butt to the tip. The stick should now be perfectly square with a nice, even taper. Test it by resting the tip end on the floor and bending it from the butt end. Note the arch it takes and see if it resumes its original shape when the pressure is released. If it does, the elasticity of the material is as it should be, but if it remains bent or takes "set," the wood is very likely to be imperfectly seasoned and the rod should be hung up in a warm closet, or near the kitchen stove, for a few weeks, to season.

To facilitate the work of planing the stick to shape, a length of pine board with a groove in one edge will be found handy. A 5-foot length of the ordinary tongue-and-groove board, about one inch thick, will be just the thing. As the tip of the rod is smaller than the butt, plane the groove in the board to make it gradually shallower to correspond to the taper of the rod. Nail this board, with the groove uppermost, to the edge of the workbench, and place the rod in the groove with one of the square corners up, which can be easily taken off with the finely set plane. Plane off the other three corners in a like manner, transforming the square stick into one of octagon form. This part of the work should be carefully done, and the stick frequently calipered at each 6-inch mark, to obtain the proper taper. It is important to make each of the eight sides as nearly uniform as the caliper and eye can do it. Set the cutter of the small plane very fine, lay the strip in the groove and plane off the corner the full length of the stick, then turn another corner uppermost and plane it off, and so on, until the stick is almost round and tapering gradually from the mark of the hand grasp to the tip.

To make the rod perfectly round, use the steel scraper in which the grooves were filed and scrape the whole rod to remove any flat or uneven spots, and finish up by sandpapering it down smooth.

The action of the rod differs with the material used, and in trying out the action, it is well to tie on the tip and guides and affix the reel by a string in order to try a few casts. If the action seems about right, give the rod a final smoothing down with No. 0 sandpaper.

For the hand grasp nothing is so good as solid cork, and while hand grasps may be purchased assembled, it is a simple matter to make them.

In Fig. 7 are shown four kinds of handles, namely, a wood sleeve, or core, A, bored to fit the butt of the rod and shaped for winding the fishing cord; a built-up cork grasp, B, made by cementing cork washers over a wood sleeve, or directly to the butt of the rod; a can-wound grip, C, mostly used for saltwater fishing; and the double-wound grip, D, made in one piece, then sawed apart in the center, the forward grip being glued in place after the reel seat is in position.

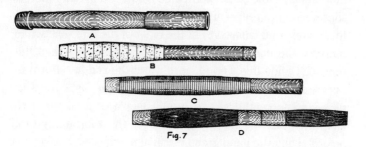

Fig. 7

To make a grip, select a number of cork washers, which may be obtained from dealers in the wholesale drug trade, or from any large fishing-tackle dealer. Make a tool for cutting a hole in their centers from a piece of tubing, or an old ferrule of the required diameter, by filing one edge sharp, then covering the other end with several thicknesses of cloth. Turn this tube around in the cork like a wad cutter. If the cutter is sharp, a nice clean cut will result, but the opposite will likely occur if an attempt is made to hammer the tube through the cork.

Having cut the butt end of the rod off square, about 1 inch from the end, or enough to remove the holes, smear a little hot glue on the end, drop a cork washer over the tip of the rod, and work it down to the butt. Cut another cork, give the first one a coat of glue, slip the former over the tip, and press the two together, and so on, until about ten corks have been glued together in position. This will give a hand grasp a trifle over 5 inches long.

A sleeve will be needed for the reel seat to slip over, and a softwood core of this sort can be purchased from any dealer in rod-making materials, or it can be made at home. For the material procure a piece of white pine, about ¾ inch in diameter and 5 inches long. A section sawed from a discarded curtain roller will serve the purpose well. Bore a ¹⁵⁄₃₂-inch hole through the piece and plane down the outside until it slips inside the reel seat. It should be well made and a good fit, and one end tapered to fit the taper of the reel seat, while the opposite end should be about ¼ inch shorter than the reel seat. Slide this wood sleeve down the rod, as shown in Fig. 8, coat the rod and the upper part of the last cork with glue, and force the sleeve tightly in place. A day or two should be allowed for the glue to set and thoroughly dry, before giving the hand grasp the final touches.

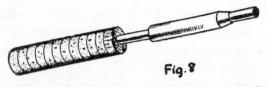

**Fig. 8**

The Corks Glued in Place on the Butt and the Wood
Sleeve, or Reel-Seat Core, Ready to Slide
Down and Glue in Position

If a lathe is at hand, the hand grasp may be turned to any desired shape, but most anglers prefer a cylindrical-shaped grip, leaving the top cork untrimmed to form a kind of shoulder when the metal reel seat is pressed into the cork. If corks of 1¼-inch diameter are purchased, little trimming will be necessary to work the hand grasp down to 1 1/16 inch in diameter. This size seems to fit the average hand about right. The lower corks will need a little trimming to fit the taper of the butt cap so that it may fit snugly in place. Cement the butt cap in place by heating the cap moderately hot, then rub a little of the melted ferrule cement inside the cap, and force it over the cork butt. When the cement has hardened, drive a small brass pin or brad through the cap, and file the ends off flush with the metal surface. All the guides, ferrules, and reel seat are shown in Fig. 9.

The regulation metal reel seat is about 4½ inches long, and in fitting it to the old type of bait rod, the covered hood is affixed to the upper end of the reel seat. This arrangement is satisfactory enough for the 9-foot bait rod, but it is rather awkward in fitting it to the short bait-casting rod, as with the hood at the upper end the reel is pushed so far forward that it leaves 1 inch or more of the reel seat exposed, and the

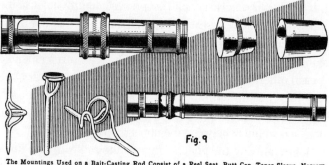

*Fig. 9*

The Mountings Used on a Bait-Casting Rod Consist of a Reel Seat, Butt Cap, Taper Sleeve, Narrow Agate Guide, Agate Offset Top, One Ring Guide, and a Welted, Shouldered Ferrule

hand must grip this smooth metal instead of the cork. To avoid this, it is best to cut the reel seat down to 3 ⅞ inches and affix the reel seat to the rod with the hood at the lower end near the hand. For a single hand grasp, a tapered winding check will be needed to make a neat finish, and this should be ordered of the correct diameter to fit the reel seat at the lower end and the diameter of the rod at the other. In the double hand grasp the winding check is used to finish off the upper end of the cork, which is tapering to fit the rod at this point.

In assembling the reel seat, push it with the hooded end well down and work it into the cork to make a tight waterproof joint. Push the reel seat up the rod, coat the sleeve with cement, and push the reel seat home. Drive a small pin through the hooded end and reel seat to make the whole rigid. This pin should not be driven through the rod or it will weaken it at this point. Just let it enter the wood a short distance to prevent the reel seat from turning.

The upper or double grasp is fashioned after the reel seat is in position, and the corks are cemented on and pushed tightly together in the same manner as used in forming the lower grasp. The first cork should be pressed tightly against the upper end of the reel seat and turned about so that the metal may enter the cork and form a tight joint. As many corks as are required to form a grip of proper length are in turn cemented to each other and the rod. After the glue has become dry, the cork may be worked down and tapered to make a smooth, swelled grasp. The winding check is now cemented on, to make a neat finish between the upper grip and the rod.

Before affixing the guides, go over the rod with fine sandpaper, then wet the wood to raise the grain, and repeat this operation, using old sandpaper. If an extrafine polish is wanted, rub it down with powdered pumice and oil, or rottenstone and oil, and finish off with an oiled rag.

To fit the agate tip, file down the end of the rod with a fine-cut file until it is a good fit in the metal tube. Melt a little of the ferrule cement and smear a little on the tip of the rod, then push the agate down in place.

Spar varnish is often used to protect the rod, but extralight coach varnish gives a better gloss, and it is as durable and waterproof as any varnish. It is only necessary to purchase a quarter pint of the varnish, as a very small quantity is used. The final varnishing is, of course, done after the rod has been wound and the guides are permanently whipped in position. However, it is an excellent idea to fill the pores of the wood by rubbing it over with a cloth saturated in the varnish before the silk whippings are put on. Merely fill the cells of the wood and wipe off all surplus, leaving the rod clean and smooth.

The guides may now be fastened in place, and for the 5-foot rod, but two of them are necessary. The first guide should be placed 19½ inches from the metal taper that finishes off the upper hand grasp, and the second guide spaced 15½ inches from the first. By spacing the guides in this manner, the line will run through them with the least possible friction.

## Winding, or Whipping, the Rod

Before whipping on the guides, take a fine file and round off the sharp edges of the base to prevent the possibility of the silk being cut. Measure off the required distances at which the guides are to be affixed, and fasten them in position by winding with a few turns of common thread. Ordinary silk of No. A size may be used, but No. 00 is the best for small rods. Most anglers agree that the size of the silk to use for the whippings should be in proportion to the size of the rod—heavy silk for the heavy rod, and fine silk for the small rod. Size A is the finest silk commonly stocked in the stores, but one or more spools of No. 00 and No. 0 may be ordered from any large dealer in fishing tackle. As a rule, size 0 gives a more workmanlike finish to the butt and joints of fly and bait rods, while No. 00 is about right to use for winding the tips. In fact, all rods weighing up to 6 ounces may be whipped with No. 00 size.

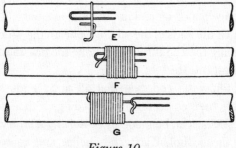

*Figure 10*

In whipping the rod, the so-called invisible knot is used. Begin the whipping, as shown at E, Fig 10, by tucking the end under the first coil and holding it with the left thumb. The spool of silk is held in the right hand and the rod is turned to the left, sufficient tension being kept on the silk so that it can be evenly coiled with each strand tightly against the other. A loop of silk, some four inches long, is well waxed and placed so that its end will project a short distance beyond the last coil which finishes the whipping. This detail is shown at F. In whipping on guides, begin the whipping at the base and work over the pointed end of the flange, winding on sufficient silk to extend about ⅛ inch beyond the pointed flange of the guide base. When the last coil is made, cut off the thread from the spool and tuck the end under the whipping by pulling on the ends of the waxed loop, as shown at G. Cut off the end neatly with a sharp knife.

For colors, bright red and a medium shade of apple green are the best, since these colors keep their original tint after varnishing, and are less likely to fade than the more delicate shades. Red finished off with a narrow circle of green always looks well, and red with yellow is likewise a good combination. Narrow windings look much better than wide whippings, and a dozen turns make about as wide a winding as the angler desires. For edgings, three or four turns of silk are about right, and these should be put on after the wider windings have been whipped on and in the same manner, although it is best to tuck the ends of the edging beneath the wider winding when pulling the end through to make the invisible knot.

**Varnishing the Rod**

After winding the rod, see that all fuzzy ends are neatly clipped off, then go over the silk windings with a coat of shellac. The shellac can be made by dissolving a little white shellac in grain alcohol. Warm the shellac and apply it with a small camel's-hair brush, giving the silk only two light coats. Allow the rod to stand a couple of days for the shellac to become thoroughly dry.

A small camel's-hair brush will be required for the varnishing—one about ½ inch wide will do. If the varnishing is to be done out of doors, a clear and warm day should be selected, and the can of coach varnish should be placed in a pot of hot water for five minutes, so that the varnish will spread evenly.

## Various Two- and Three-Piece Rods

While the action of the one-piece rod is undeniably better than when the rod is made in two or three pieces, it is less compact to carry. To make a five-foot two-piece bait-casting rod, the same dimensions as given for the one-piece rod will make a very fine fishing tool. It is well to make two tips in view of a possible breakage. The rod may consist of two pieces of equal length, but a rod of better action is secured by making the butt section somewhat shorter with a relatively longer tip. By making the butt section about 23 inches long, exclusive of ferrule and butt cap, and the tip section 32½ inches long, a splendid little rod is obtained that will fit any of the regulation rod cases of 35-inch length. To make a 6½-ounce rod of this kind with a cork hand grasp, caliper it in the same manner as the one-piece rod, making the butt section 32½ inches long, tapering from $^{15}/_{32}$ inch at the upper end of the hand grasp to $^{19}/_{64}$ inch at the ferrule. The tip is made 33 inches long, tapering from $^{17}/_{64}$ inch to $^{7}/_{64}$ inch. By making the tip and butt to these lengths, both parts will be of equal length when the ferrules and the tops are added. The material list is as follow, the attachments being made of German silver:

Dagame or greenheart butt, ⅝ inch by 3 feet long.
Two tips ⅜ inch by 3 feet long.
One ¾-inch reel seat with straight hood.
One 1-inch butt cap.

One taper, $^{15}/_{32}$ inch at the small end.
Two $^{3}/_{32}$-inch offset agate tops.
Two $^{1}/_{2}$-inch narrow agate guides.
Two No. 1 size one-ring casting guides.
One $^{17}/_{64}$ inch welted and shouldered ferrule,
    with two closed-end centers, one for each tip.
Two dozen cork washers, $1^{1}/_{4}$ inches in diameter.
Two spools of winding silk.

The three-piece rod should be make up to 6 feet in length
to secure the best action, but even if so made, the use of the
extra ferrules makes the rod less resilient and elastic than
the rod of one- or two-piece construction. The best action is
obtained only when the rod bends to a uniform curve, and
since the ferrules cannot conform to this curve, or arc, the
more joints incorporated in a rod, the less satisfactory it will
be from an angling standpoint. Convenience in packing and
carrying are the sole merits which the many-jointed rod possesses. Complete specifications for making a three-piece
bait-casting rod, together with a material list, is as follows:

A rod, about $5^{1}/_{2}$ feet long with a single or double hand
grasp made of cork, will weigh about 7 ounces. Caliper
the butt so that it will taper from $^{15}/_{32}$ inch to $^{11}/_{32}$ inch at
the cap of the ferrule, making it $21^{1}/_{2}$ inches long. The
middle joint is tapered from $^{21}/_{64}$ inch to $^{15}/_{64}$ inch, and is
$21^{3}/_{4}$ inches long. The tips are 21 inches long and are
tapered from $^{13}/_{64}$ inch to $^{7}/_{64}$ inch.
Dagame or greenheart is used for the butt, joint, and
tips, and German silver for the fittings. All pieces are 2
feet long, the butt is $^{5}/_{8}$ inch, the joint and tips, $^{3}/_{8}$ inch.
One $^{3}/_{4}$-inch reel seat with straight hood.
One 1-inch butt cap.
One taper, small end $^{15}/_{32}$ inch.
One $^{21}/_{64}$-inch welted and shouldered ferrule.

One $^{15}/_{64}$-inch welted and shouldered ferrule with two
   closed centers, one for each tip.
Two $^{3}/_{32}$ -inch offset agate tops.
Two $^{1}/_{2}$-inch narrow agate guides.
Two No. 1 size one-ring casting guides.
Two dozen cork washers.
Winding silk, size 00 or 0.

## Fly Rods for Trout and Bass

Having made a good bait-casting rod, the amateur will find
little trouble in making a rod with a number of joints, and no
special instructions need be given, since the work of planing and smoothing up the wood, and finishing and mounting the rod, is the same as has been described in detail
before.

For fly-fishing for trout, accuracy and delicacy are of more
importance than length of cast, and the rod best suited to
this phase of angling differs greatly from that used in bait
casting. A stiff, heavy rod is entirely unsuited for fly-casting,
and while it is, of course, possible to make a rod too willowy
for the sport, the amateur, working by rule of thumb, is more
likely to err on the other side and make the fly rods of too
stout a caliber. The idea is simply to help the amateur over
the hard part by giving a list of dimensions of a representative trout and a bass fly rod.

To make a 9-foot trout fly rod, with a cork grasp having a
length of 9 inches above the reel seat, caliper the material as
follows:

The butt is tapered from $^{7}/_{16}$ inch to $^{25}/_{64}$ inch at 1 foot
from the butt end; 1½ feet, $^{11}/_{32}$ inch; 2 feet, $^{21}/_{64}$ inch; 2½
feet, $^{5}/_{16}$ inch; and 3 feet, $^{19}/_{64}$ inch.
The first 6 inches of the middle joint is calipered to $^{9}/_{32}$
inch; 1 foot, $^{17}/_{64}$ inch; 1½ feet, $^{15}/_{64}$ inch; 2 feet, $^{7}/_{32}$ inch;
2½ feet, $^{13}/_{64}$ inch; and 3 feet, $^{3}/_{16}$ inch.

The first 6 inches of the tips are calipered to ¹¹⁄₆₄ inch; 1 foot, ⁵⁄₃₂ inch; 1½ feet, ⅛ inch; 2 feet, ⁷⁄₆₄ inch; 2½ feet, ³⁄₃₂ inch; and 3 feet, ⁵⁄₆₄ inch.

All joints are made 36½ inches long.

The material used is dagame, or greenheart, the butt being ⅝ inch by 4 feet, the joint ⅜ inch by 4 feet, and the tips ⅜ inch by 4 feet The attachments, of German silver, are:

One ¾-inch reel seat, fly-rod type with butt cap.

One taper, ³³⁄₆₄ inch at the small end.

One ⁹⁄₃₂-inch welted and shouldered ferrule.

One ¹¹⁄₆₄-inch welted and shouldered ferrule with two closed-end centers, one for each tip.

Two No. 4 snake guides for the middle joint, and six No. 2 snake guides, three for each tip section.

Two No. 7 agate angle fly tops, the kind to wind on.

One dozen cork washers.

Two 10-yard spools of winding silk, 00 size.

A bass fly rod 9½ feet long, weighing 7½ ounces, with a cork grasp, 9½ inches above the reel seat, is calipered as follows:

The butt is tapered from ¹³⁄₃₂ inch to ²⁵⁄₆₄ inch 1 foot from the end; 1½ feet from butt, ²³⁄₆₄ inch; 2 feet, ¹¹⁄₃₂ inch ; 2½ feet, ²¹⁄₆₄ inch; and 3 feet, ¹⁹⁄₆₄ inch.

The first 6 inches of the middle joint is ¹⁹⁄₆₄ inch; 1 foot, ⁹⁄₃₂ inch; 1½ feet, ¹⁷⁄₆₄ inch; 2 feet, ¹⁵⁄₆₄ inch; 2½ feet, ⁷⁄₃₂ inch; and 3 feet, ¹⁹⁄₆₄ inch

The first 6 inches of the tips, ¹¹⁄₆₄ inch; 1 foot, ⁵⁄₃₂ inch; 1½ feet, ⁹⁄₆₄ inch; 2 feet, ⅛ inch; 2½ feet, ⁷⁄₆₄ inch; and 3 feet, ⁵⁄₆₄ inch.

The joints are 36½ inches long. The mountings are the same as for the trout fly rod. Dagame, or greenheart, wood is used, the butt being ⅝ inch by 4 feet, the joint ⅜ inch by 4 feet, and the tips ⅜ inch by 4 feet.

The two-piece saltwater rod with an 18-inch double cork hand grasp, the whole being 6½ feet long, is made to weigh about 13 ounces, with the following caliperings:

A uniform taper of ³⁵⁄₆₄ inch to ²⁹⁄₆₄ inch, from the cork grasp to the ferrule, is given to the butt.

The first 6 inches of the tips is ¹³⁄₃₂ inch; 1-foot, ²⁵⁄₆₄ inch; 1½ feet, ¹¹⁄₃₂ inch; 2 feet, ²¹⁄₆₄ inch; 2½ feet, ⁹⁄₃₂ inch; and to tip, ¹⁵⁄₆₄ inch. The joints are made 36¾ inches long. Dagame, or greenheart, is used with German-silver mountings.

Both pieces of wood are 4 feet long, the butt being of ¾ inch and the tip of ½ inch material.

One ⅞-inch reel seat with straight hood.

One 1-inch butt cap.

One ⁷⁄₁₆-inch ferrule.

One taper with small end ³⁵⁄₆₄-inch.

One ¹⁰⁄₃₂-inch stirrup-tube agate top.

Two No. 3 bell guides.

Two dozen cork washers.

Two spools, size A, winding silk.

## The Independent-Butt Rod

The independent-butt rod, in which the hand grasp contains the ferrule and the tip is made in one piece, is a favorite type with many of the best fishermen. This mode of construction may be used with all classes of rods, the light fly and bait-casting rods, and the heavier caliber rods used in saltwater angling. In rods of this type, it is only necessary to use the same size ferrule to make as many tips as desired to fit the one butt. Tips of several calibers and weights may thus be fashioned to fit the one butt, and if the single-piece tip is too long for some special use, one tip may be made a jointed one for ease in carrying.

The independent butt, or hand grasp, is made by fitting

the ferrule directly on a length of dagame, or greenheart, which has been rounded so that the seated ferrule will not touch the wood. The ferrule is then cemented and riveted in place, and a soft-pine sleeve is fitted over the wood core and the ferrule. The forward end of the sleeve is, of course, tapered to fit the taper of the reel seat, and when properly fitted, its lower end will project about ¼ inch beyond the pine sleeve. Glue the sleeve on this wood core, cement the reel seat to the sleeve, and rivet the reel seat in place.

The cork washers are glued in position, working the first one into the metal edge of the reel seat, to make a nice, tight joint at this point. The other corks are then glued in place until the hand grasp is of the desired length. The projecting end of the wood core is then cut off flush with the last cork, and the rod is mounted in the usual manner.

In making a double hand grasp, the forward grasp may be fitted over the wood core in the fashion already described in making the hand grasp for the one-piece bait-casting rod, or the forward grasp may be fitted to the tip, just above the ferrule, as preferred. Both methods are commonly used, the only difference being in the manner of finishing up the forward grasp. If the forward grip is affixed to the ferruled end of the tip, two tapered thimbles will be required to make a nice finish.

The heavy-surf, or tarpon, rod is made up of an independent, detachable butt, 20 inches long, having a solid-cork or cord-wound hand grasp, and a one-piece tip, 5½ feet long, altogether weighing 23½ ounces. It is uniformly calipered to taper from ⅔ inch to ⁵⁄₁₆ inch.

One piece of dagame, or greenheart, 1 inch by 6½ feet, will be required.
One 1-inch reel seat for detachable butt, including one ¾-inch male ferrule
One 1 ⅛-inch butt cap.

Two No. 11 wide, raised agate guides: two No. 1 trumpet guides.

One ⅜-inch agate stirrup top.

Two spools of winding silk, A-size.

Two dozen cork washers, or sufficient fish line to cord the butt.

The guides are whipped on double, the first set spaced 10 inches from the top, and the second, 26 inches from the reel. The core of the independent, or detachable, butt is constructed of the same material as the rod, which makes the hand grasp somewhat elastic and very much superior to a stiff and rigid butt.

—Stillman Taylor

## MISCELLANEOUS WRINKLES AND KINKS FOR FISHERMEN, ANGLERS, ETC.

**Keep Angle Worms Not in a Tin Can** but in a small earthen jar (very small flowerpot); fill it not with mud or dirt, but green moss, wet. If fed with the white of a hardboiled egg, placed therein, or a teaspoonful of cream or bruised celery, they will assume a pink color, live long, and be attractive. Don't drown them in mud as most do. Cover hole in bottom with a piece of pot.

**A Splendid Bait**—Are live maggots taken from meat that is flyblown. Anglers will do well not to despise the hitherto considered repulsive maggot, if kept in a small box, with cornmeal; there is no more objection to handling them, than any worm or other slimy bait; try it once and be convinced.

**In Early Spring**—Use very small midge flies when trout fishing.

**Carry and Dry Your Flies**—By sticking them under your hatband, or around it; a few dozen can be accommodated thus, keeping them safely and drying them when needed.

**Don't Use Too Big Flies or Hooks**—Better small than too large; big fish will take a small hook, but little ones can't take a large one.

**Fish Scent or Lure**—A little asafetida, oil of anise, or sweet sicily; a drop pinched in your bait will attract fish to it.

**Don't Blame the Fish**—For not biting, or taking the fly. Perhaps you're to blame. Think over conditions and inspect your bait or tackle.

**The Difficult Places**—To fish are just where the fish are.

**Old Fish**—Like new flies. Young fish like old ones.

**Advice to Landowners**—When you catch thieves please cut off all their pants *buttons*. They can't run well and hold up their pants at the same time.

**Kill Every Water Snake**—You find. They eat millions of fish eggs every year.

**To Keep Fish Alive**—Use a fish bag, even a gunnysack, with small slits on its top and center.

**To Find Worms**—Choose a manure pile or after a heavy rain, when they crawl to the surface of the ground.

**Take Your Wife**—Along on your fishing trips. She will surely enjoy it, or else take—

**Choosing Flies**—Choose the smaller ones every time.

**Flyblown Meat**—Suspended over a trout or fish hole drops the maggots continually in the water. This attracts fish to that vicinity.

**Oil Reels**—With good clock oil, not *watch* oil.

**Red Chubs**—Or black stripped minnows are excellent bait.

**To Attract Minnows**—Throw fresh meat-bone refuse in shallow waters or likely places; it keeps them hovering around it.

**Fishing at Night**—Is fishing right. Fishing midday hardly pays. Dark days are best, they say.

**Clean Utensils**—Used in cooking fish (when hot using sand and water), scouring it hard before you cook meats, vegetables, etc.

**Frogging at Night**—Take a very bright light, locate your frog, and turn the light on him squarely. It dazzles him and you can pick him up like a potato. Don't think he'll jump away; the light confuses him and he forgets himself.

**In Casting for Bass**—Choose the edge of lily pads, weeds, rushes, etc. Pickerel also.

**Fish Scratches or Wounds**—Use common salt and vinegar, or suck them well and put a chew of tobacco around it and bind it on.

**Never Let Your Shadow**—Be observed by fish you are after. Get behind a tree, bank, or cut a few branches so as to hide yourself behind them, or lie in the high grass and crawl to the most likely spots, especially in trout fishing.

**Never Use Pork Rind**—Except in trolling. Use the white fat meat instead and shape as near to either a minnow or frog as possible.

**If Wading or Your Clothes Are Wet**—Keep moving and there is no danger of a chill.

**Always Carry a File**—A small one to sharpen the barbs of your hooks. Examine them often to see that they are sharp.

**Keep Your Spoons Bright**—Revolving spoons can be scoured with tobacco ashes or wood ashes; polish them with a dry rag and elbow grease.

**Brass or Copper Spoons**—Vinegar and salt will instantly clean and brighten them if rubbed hard with a rag dipped in above, then polished with a dry one.

**To Kill Fish**—Hit them between the eyes with a club, stick of wood, knife handle, etc.

**Fish Killed at Once**—As soon as caught, keep better, and the flesh remains firmer and better all around.

**Catch Frogs**—Use hook and line, and piece of red or scarlet rag. Keep only for bait the little ones; the large ones, use their hindquarters and fry and eat them. Excellent.

**Keep Frogs**—In a perforated box, with a little moist grass, they need no water at all, and will keep in a cool place without food or drink for a week or more; simply drench them once or twice a day only.

**Keep Shrimp**—Put them in wet sawdust, moss, water grass, or seaweed.

**To Preserve Fish**—Use Preserveline. One pound will preserve 50 to 100 pounds of fish. It's all right.

**To Feed and Keep Worms Fat**—And alive, use the white of a hardboiled egg, a small part of it.

**Smear Red Ferrules**—With tallow before jointing them and they won't stick when unjointing them. If they do, apply the heat of a match so as to expand the metal.

**The Man in the Boat**—Should keep still, and aid the angler, not retard him.

**To Soften Leaders**—Soak them in vinegar and water.

**Never Use Dry Leaders**—You are apt to fracture and ruin them.

**To Keep Leaders**—Soak them in strong green or black tea or very strong coffee.

**Always Test**—Your lines, leaders, snells, etc., before starting out on a trip.

**In Purchasing Flies**—Always buy the best, even if you must economize elsewhere.

**Always Have**—An extra rod tip along with you on a trip.

**On Cold Days**—Trout are sluggish and unless hungry or feeding, refuse to bite.

**On Hot Days**—They usually await the cool evening or morning before biting well.

Astonishing insights on angling may also be found among the pages of *A Man's Life: The Complete Instructions.*

---

An Easy Way to Put a Fish Hook on a Line

Make a loop at the end of your line. Put it through the eye of the hook and over the barb as shown in the

illustration. Take hold of "A" and bring it in the direction of the arrows until it is tight at the head of the hook. To remove, simply draw the loop back over the barb.

---

**In Fishing for Black Bass**—It is next to useless to cast on perfectly smooth water.

**Use Small Spoons**—When trolling for bass.

**Black Bass**—Go in pairs all summer. If you catch one look out for its mate.

**In Trolling for Bass**—Row about three miles an hour only; the tendency in trolling is to go too fast. Row only to keep good motion of your bait, and, if you twitch it often so as to make it spurt or swerve, so much the better.

**In Fishing with Live Bait**—Allow time for the fish to turn and swallow or gorge the bait, as fish invariable swallow bait fish head first. If using minnows keep them well under water. In rapid waters, it will by its own force unless sinkered; keep the minnow near the surface, which is the proper way.

**A Little Red or Colored Rag**—Fastened at the head of spoon bait often makes a more attractive lure.

**Use a Fish Scaler**—For cleaning or scaling all fish.

**For Weak Fish**—Use a pearl weak fish squid bait.

**For Large Bass or Trout**—Use a good spinner fly.

**Fish in Spawning Season**—Are less apt to be scared, yet there are many who absolutely refuse any food at these times; before or after they will eagerly take anything offered them.

**The Largest Fish**—Can ofttimes be found in most shallow or unlikely waters in search of food.

**Always Buy**—The very best flies that money can purchase, and provide yourself with abundant select bait, even if you must travel third class to do it, for the first-class fishing will result.

**To Use Frog Successfully**—Keep or move so as to resemble life, a twitching movement is best (as a frog swims).

**Brook Trout**—In autumn (spawning season) take no food.

**Good Bass Flies**—Jungle Cock, Silver Doctor, Montreal, Frank, Henry, Coachman, Epting, Seth Green, Ferguson, Lord Baltimore.

**If a String**—Is in a knot, patience will untie it; patience does most anything if you will but try it.

**March**—This is the earliest time for fly-fishing, and can only be practical when the snow water is all out of streams. The earliest fly found on waters is the February Red, Blue Dun, March Brown.

**April**—Red Spinner, Cow Dung, Red and Black Hackles, Iron Blue and Yellow Dun.

**May**—Stone Fly, Sedge Fly, Alden Fly, Black Gnat, Evening Dun.

**June**—(Best month for trout.) Green Drake or May Fly, Grey Drake, Choh-y-bon-Dhu (try it), Brachen, Shorn Fly, Light, Colored Duns, and spinners.

**July**—(The worst month.) White and Brown Moths, Red and Black Ant Flies, and Small Midges.

**August**—August Dun and Cinnamon Whirling Dun and Willow Fly, bringing up the angler's season for fly-fishing for trout.

**Use Cork Handles**—To your rods. They are softer, cooler to the hands.

**Be Cautious**—More caution is required in fly-fishing than in bait fishing; objects beneath the water do not scare fish so easily as those on the surface.

**Fish Take Live Bait**—When fish seize smaller fish, they always swallow it head first, so give it time to turn and gorge it thus, before you strike.

**To Extract Hooks**—From flesh or clothing, push back the upper end so as to bring point out where it went in.

**Best Bass Fishing**—Is at night or on a cloudy day, or early morn or evening.

**Strew Ferns**—In your fish basket or creel, to keep trout separate, clean, and moist.

**For Fly-Casting**—Use a very light elastic or flexible rod, strong and serviceable, six to nine feet in length, not over six ounces in weight.

**For Bait Fishing**—Use a medium-weight, fairly stiff rod, about nine feet long.

**For Trolling**—Use a short stiff rod, extremely stout and strong, six to eight feet long, weighing twelve ounces or more.

**For Salmon Fishing**—Use a double handed rod, fifteen feet long, about fifteen ounces.

**The Eyes of Fish**—Are peculiarly placed rendering him incapable of seeing plainly objects on a level or directly under him. They can, however, see plainly all that is going on above, and for a long distance about him, say forty to fifty feet.

**Fish Don't Bite**—Always to satisfy hunger only. They often strike at a glittering or attractive bait for pure viciousness or greediness.

**Always Breakfast**—Before starting out mornings "a-fishing." Don't start out on an empty stomach, or *too early*.

**A Fish Decoy**—Take a dozen bright minnows, and cork them up in a bottle (a clear glass one) of water with a small hole in the cork; suspend them midwater, in a very likely spot; when the bottle is submerged, it is hid by the color of the glass and water, and the imprisoned but moving minnows attract other fish to that vicinity.

**Keep Minnows Alive**—By providing or attaching to your minnow pail a rubber tube and air bulb. Fill the bulb with air and force it through the tube into the water, thus "aerating it" or supplying air to the water. Thus you have the most expensive minnow pail, at a cost of a few cents.

**In Bottom or Still Fishing**—Plumb the depth of the water first, so as to be sure of its depth; then act accordingly.

**Excellent Bait for Bass**—Young carp, very small green frogs, live grasshoppers.

**In Fastening Frogs**—Pass the hook through both lips and use the smaller ones.

**For Carp Fishing**—White maggots smeared with honey, stale doughy sweetened bread, potatoes, etc. Wait until he swims away with the bait before you strike.

**The Best Time**—For trout fishing is at night when large fish are active. Select a quiet spot near a deep hole, and leave it for a night trial. Cut a few branches and group them around so as to hide yourself behind them. Do this the day before you fish the spot. Cast over and draw your bait or fly quietly over the top of the water. If big trout are there you'll quickly get a rise.

**Don't Fry Trout**—Try broiling it over the campfire.

**Bait Casting**—Use a short rod five to seven feet long, a fine, smooth line, free-running quadruple reel. Wind the line until the bait is close to the rod, then cast as you would throw an apple from a pointed stick. Cast the bait fifty to sixty feet or more from the boat, which should be in deep water, and casts made toward shallow water. Cast to the edges of the rushes, weeds, etc., then troll the bait to the boat for the recast.

**Repair Kit**—For anglers, containing awls, brads, shellac mending silk, wax, cement, etc., should be taken on long trips.

**For Cold Weather**—Use a chamois shirt; light and warm as a coat. They are flannel lined.

**A Splendid Fish Bait**—Maggots from meat that has been flyblown.

**Lead Your Hook**—Well to head of live fish bait.

**To Preserve a Landing Net**—Immerse it in linseed oil. Shake it out well, stretch it open, and dry well.

**Yellow Perch**—Like gay-colored trout hackles if sunk below the surface. Use one or more flies at the same time.

**Dead Sand Worms**—Are useless for bait in saltwater fishing.

**In Trout Fishing**—If you can't hide behind places, cut a tree branch or two and make a blind. Do this the day before you fish that spot.

**Hide from View**—I have seen a dozen fish leap to take the fly, but the moment they caught sight of me they refused everything later offered them; a few hours later I took care to hide myself and crawl cautiously near that spot. The finest fishing I have enjoyed resulted from that care.

**In Your Tackle Box**—Should be a stick of angler's wax and ferrule or rod cement, a few connecting links, split buckshot, a weedless floating meadow frog, for casting; a spinning fly for casting or trolling; other trolling baits, spoons, etc.; a gimp leader, a bucktail bass fly and spoon; a double and single swivel, a foul tackle clearing ring, a bank sinker, a cork float, and a fisherman's file and pliers, and if possible a line dryer, leader box, and fly book and you have an outfit that is complete.

**Consult Your Guide**—If possible, follow his recommendations, treat him with the same respect as you expect from him, insist upon his doing his duty thoroughly and well, always take a receipt for money paid.

**Double Barb Hooks**—Can be purchased any size, and are used for fish that nibble instead of biting.

**Don't Strike Too Hard**—Approach likely waters carefully and fish the nearest side first; when you rise a good fish and fail to hook him, give him a little rest before casting over him again.

**Notice What Flies**—Are on the waters you are fishing and what the fish seem to be taking, and imitate it.

**Open the Stomach**—Of your first fish and see what they are feeding on, and follow the "tip."

**Use a Smaller Fly**—Than the natural one; the larger the imitation the easier fish can observe the fraud.

**For Trolling**—Troll close to the edge of rushes, lily pads, etc., just between deep and shallow or light and dark waters. Morning, evening, and after dark is the best times for trolling.

**Using Spinners**—Go slow and deep for success and big fish.

**On Wet Days**—Fish often fail to bite because food is washed into the waters in plenty.

**In Bait or Fly-Fishing**—Always fish downstream. There are times, however, that upstream has its advantages, but it's hard work.

**Fish Cannot be Caught**—While snow water is in streams.

**Grub Worms**—Make good bait.

**Change Your Flies**—Often if fish refuse to rise; fish that ofttimes refuse seasonable flies will strike eagerly at a most radical change.

**Keep the Sun**—In front of or at the side of you when fishing.

**It is Said**—Fish bite better between the new moon and first quarter.

**On Cloudy Days**—Use bright flies, dark days use white flies, bright days use dark flies.

**A Nest of Very Small Mice**—Make excellent large trout or bass bait.

**Fish Decoy**—Cut up small fish, meats, etc., and scatter in likely still waters the day before you fish there. It will attract them to that vicinity.

**Salmon Leaders**—Should be nine feet long. Trout leaders, six feet long.

**Bobbing for Eels**—Take a piece of stout darning worsted and a needle and thread it full of angle worms; the longer the string the better. Wind it up in loops, tie your line to it, and sink it to the bottom, where the eels are (do this at night). When they bite, their teeth get caught in the worsted and holds them fast; or take a piece of raw meat and sew it full of worsted, cross and recross, and it will answer the same purpose.

**Good Saltwater Bait**—Shrimps, shedder, crabs, sand worms, clams (hard portion), small crawfish, etc.

**A Tangled, Kinky Line**—Can be unraveled by towing it behind a boat or trailing it in running water.

**Raw Beef or Raw Liver**—Especially hog's liver is excellent spring bait.

**To Skin Eels**—Pin with a fork his tail to a tree stump, split the skin around a few inches from the fork, and pull it over his head. *Fry or stew them*.

**Asafetida**—Or camphor put in bait box is said to attract fish by its scent.

**In Fly-Casting**—Have the wind at your back, the sun before you, and do not let your line touch the water; that's the place for your fly only.

**Keep Minnows Alive**—Or revive them by adding a spoonful of salt to the water.

**A Live Chub**—Makes good bass bait, or use the Dobson or Helgramite. Find in brooks and rivers under large stones.

**The Best Time**—For trout, the month of June.

**When Bass or Trout**—Refuse to rise to the surface for a fly, try sinking it a foot below the surface.

**Fish in the Water**—Can see plainly out of it. Things in the water are magnified out of it, just as they are magnified in the water for you.

**When Wading**—Tie strings to articles in your pockets, lest they fall out in the water and *be lost*.

**Tie Your Hat**—To your back shirt collar with a piece of cord (out of the way) for windy days.

**Fish Early**—And fish late. It is a good plan midday or hot noons to take a *rest* or choose shady spots and deep waters.

**Carry a Mosquito Hat**—It's worth its price, in an hour at times. Get it folding and pocket size.

**No Fisherman or Angler**—Should fail to provide himself with a copy of the Fish and Game Laws of the United States. Price 24 cents, post paid.

**Don't Wash Fish**—When desired to keep them any length of time; simply draw and wipe them dry.

**For Stream Fishing**—Use size G or H line; for lake fishing use F or G line; for still fishing use G or H line.

**In Fishing from a Boat**—Use adjustable rod holders, which can be adjusted to any angle on side or seat of the boat.

**Bucktail Bass Flies**—Are made from the hair of a deer (buck) tail, the hair of which does not mat when wet. Bodies are of pure silk ribbed with tinsel tied on hollow sproat hooks.

**Good Trout Flies**—Brown Hackle, Parmacheene Belle, Montreal, Silver Doctor.

**For Tarpon Fishing**—Use a stiff rod 6 feet long (double handed).

**For Bait Fishing**—Use a rod 6 to 10 feet long, 5 to 10 ounces.

**For Fly-Fishing**—7 to 9 feet long, 5 to 8 ounces.

**For Bait Casting**—6 to 9 feet long, 5 to 8 ounces.

**For Trolling**—(If a rod is used) 6 to 8 feet long, 12 ounces or more.

**All Round Rod**—A combination (two rods in one) of a two-piece bait or trolling rod and a three-piece fly and casting rod making both, a 7 foot and 9½ foot rod.

When desired steel telescopic or jointed rods can be furnished. Valise or trunk rods of any well-known woods used in the manufacture of standard rods. Lancewood, greenheart in two-, three-, four-, five-, or six-piece rods (any length, any weight) or six- or eight-strip hexagonal split bamboo (finest rods made) made, if desired, especially to your order. Spiral or twisted split bamboo or silkien invisible rods made to order.

**Build a Large Bonfire**—Where the reflection can be cast upon and about the waters. It will attract fish at night to that vicinity.

**South and West Winds**—Are said by fishermen to be the best winds for fishing.

**A Pocket Fish Scale**—Will correctly tell the weight of your capture. Weigh as soon as removed from water, as they loose weight after.

**Bass, Pike, Pickerel**—When feeding, are alert toward shores or shallow waters.

**In Trout Fishing**—Use a lively grasshopper. Get behind a tree or bank and crawl unseen to a very likely spot. Drop it in gently and move it on the surface (as if alive) and you will have sport, if they abound there.

**Practice Fly-Casting**—In natural waters. Aim not for distance but perfection.

**Dye Your Leaders**—Mist color, using one dram of logwood, six grains copperas, boiled in one pint of water. Immerse leaders for five minutes or until correct color is obtained.

**Oil of Rhodium**—A few drops on your bait when fishing with a hook, and fish will never refuse to bite. Add a little of this to bait on small game traps, or oil of amber and oil of rhodium mixed (equal parts), or beaver oil, and the odor will attract them from afar; their scent of this is remarkable and they will risk anything to secure it.

These are reliable secrets of most noted trappers, and the above has been the Chinese secret of catching fish for centuries.

**Wipe Your Lines**—With a sponge or cotton rag so as to absorb the moisture when through fishing, or unreel and dry them when you get to camp.

**Port and Starboard**—"Port" is the left-hand side of a boat (looking forward); "starboard" to right side; "windward" the side the wind comes from; "leeward," the other side; "ahead," in front of the boat; "astern," in rear of the boat; "abeam," off the center of boat, for instance, port or starboard quarter; "amidships," center of boat.

Consult the instructions in Appendix I to learn how a canoe may be made of paper and the best way to construct a basic skiff.

## SUGGESTIONS FOR OUTFITS

Our advice above on how to construct your own fishing outfit is most useful. Of course, not every man has the time or skill to make his own fishing rod. For these men, we offer these following suggestions. They are subject to change as per the individual fancy and likes of the user or intending purchaser.

### A Common Yet Practical Outfit (for Still Fishing)

A bamboo pole, 10 to 12 feet long with reel.
25 to 50 yards silk or linen line size G or F.
A common cork float, split shot sinkers.
2 three-foot leaders, silk worm gut.
A few No. 6–7–8–9 sproat hooks (snelled).
A fish stringer and bait box.

### A Simple Trolling Outfit

100 yards of stout linen line and reel, hook and sinker, one assortment of spoon baits for trolling.
1 weedless trolling spoon and leader.

### Outfit for Trout, Bass, Pike, Pickerel, Etc., Etc.

8 foot lancewood rod, extra tip and case, multiplier reel with click.
25 to 50 yards of stout silk line.
100 yards trolling line and reel.
3 six-foot gut leaders.

2 dozen very best trout and bass flies (special).
2 trout and bass spinners or spoons.
3 casting baits, minnow, frog, and bucktail, weedless.
½ dozen assorted hooks, sinkers, and swivels.
  1 landing net, creel, straps, and bait box.

---

### An All-Around Fine Outfit

1 first-class combination rod (bait and fly sizes
    two in one).
1 quadruple multiplying reel, with click in case.
50 yards of fine fly-casting line, all silk.
100 yards of all linen braided, trolling line (on
    reel complete).
½ dozen assorted sizes silkworm gut leaders.
1 adjustable float (split-shot sinkers and swivels).
1 bank or casting sinker.
1 dozen assorted sizes sproat hooks.
1 fly book with 3 dozen assorted finest flies, "spe-
    cial."
6 assorted spinners and spoon baits, plain and
    weedless.
3 assorted casting baits, plain and weedless.
1 landing net, Harrimac or equal.
1 tackle and bait box.
1 creel and straps; 1 minnow pail.

# The Sporting Rifle

❦

Sportsmen are interested in rifles and rifle shooting largely from the hunting standpoint, although target shooting is a favorite sport with many of them. This discussion of the sporting rifle will be concerned, therefore, principally with the hunting aspects, other forms of shooting being considered as good methods of practice and the development of skill in the use of hunting weapons. The novice, as well as the good shot, must have a suitable weapon, and should have at least a general knowledge of the types of rifles available, and their common uses. A number of representative types of rifles are shown in Fig. 1, and the details of the breech mechanisms and sights in Fig. 2. The full-page illustration shows several positions in the use of the rifle; a moving-target arrangement, to be constructed by the trajectory of a rifle bullet; and several diagrams of the vital shots in hunting common big game.

The single-shot rifle, shown at A, Fig. 1, has been largely supplanted by the repeater and the automatic, so far as hunting is concerned. For use exclusively in indoor shooting, a heavy rifle of the "Schuetzen" type is best suited. A high-grade ornamented rifle of this type is shown in the headpiece of this article.

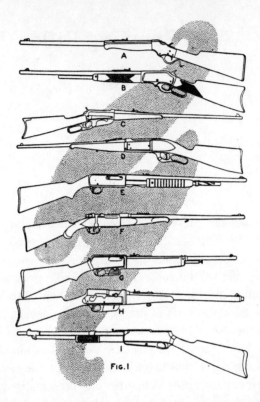

Fig. 1

The most popular type of American rifle is the repeater or the lever-action variety, shown at B. The lever action embodies many good points: quickness of fire, ease of operation, freedom from jamming at a critical moment, strength, and plenty of stopping power. Several types of lever-action rifles are shown in Fig. 1.

Almost all lever-action repeaters are of the tubular-magazine type, the magazine extending under the barrel, sometimes the full length—full magazine; or halfway—half magazine. Rifles of these types are shown at B and C, and a hammerless repeater at D.

The trombone, or pump-action, repeating rifle, shown at E, has a mechanism similar to that used in the repeating shotgun, the sliding forearm loading and ejecting the cartridge. The merit of the military bolt-action rifle lies in its great strength and simplicity. A weapon of this type was used by Roosevelt in Africa, and by other big-game hunters. It is shown at F.

The chief advantages of the automatic rifle, shown at G, which is a comparatively new weapon, are its speed in firing and its almost noiseless action. This rifle has a recoil-operated action of the blowback type. That shown at H has a box magazine, and the automatic action is based on the sliding of the barrel within a steel jacket. The rifle shown at I may be used either as an automatic or as a pump-action weapon.

The subject of stock and trigger adjustment is one to which every experienced rifleman devotes considerable attention. The regular stock rifle is built to standard dimensions, and often the stock is found a trifle short. For the man of average reach, a 13¾-inch stock, with a 1⅞-inch drop at the comb, and about 3-inch drop at the heel, will be found satisfactory.

Rifle sights are of several types, of which there are in turn many variations. Only the essentials of the standard types will be considered. The regulation open sights, with which most rifles are fitted at the factory, are the buckhorn rear and the Rocky Mountain front sight. For a hunting rifle the most satisfactory sights are a gold-bead front sight of about ³⁄₂₂-inch diameter, a folding-leaf rear sight, and a combination rear aperture sight, mounted on the tang of the rifle. An arm so sighted is useful for all kinds of shooting. The combination rear sight is used in deliberate shots at a target or at game, and the folding-leaf sight is better than the buckhorn for quick snap-shooting.

The sportsman who wishes to master the use of a rifle must have a knowledge of the trajectory of such weapons, and particularly of the rifle he uses regularly. He must know, also, how to align the sights correctly to get satisfactory results. The trajectory is the path that the rifle bullet takes in passing from the muzzle of the rifle to its mark. The force of gravity acts upon the bullet in flight, and the result is that the trajectory is curved, as indicated in the diagram at the bottom of the page illustration. A relatively low trajectory is, of course, desirable in a hunting rifle. The black-powder, or slow speed, cartridge has a relatively high trajectory, while the high-power smokeless cartridges have relatively low trajectories.

The adjustment of the sights of a rifle is also of much importance. Every rifle is targeted at the factory, but this may be done by a fair shot, using the following method: Arrange three boxes, so that the rifle barrel may rest upon one, and the arms of the marksman upon the other two. Place a bag of sand upon the box, so that the barrel may rest upon it, about six inches from the muzzle. Put the target into place, and adjust the sights for 100 yards. If the sights are properly lined up, the shots should fall quite regularly within a ten-inch circle. With peep, or other target, sights, much finer results will be obtained. In moving the sights it must be remembered that to move the rear sight to the right will bring the shot to the right, and vice versa, while if the front sight is moved to the right, the arm will shoot to the left. In making the test, first adjust the front sight so that it is in exact alignment with the center of the barrel, and then all corrections may be made by moving the rear sight.

The proper way to sight a rifle is to hold the front sight just clear of the notch in the rear sight, with the front bead barely touching the outer ring of the bull's-eye, at the extreme bottom. It is the rule of good rifle shot to "see day-light between the sight and the bull's-eye." In any event, do not cover up the front sight by drawing it down into the notch of the rear sight, so that only the top of the bead is visible. Another frequent error is to hold the front sight to cover the bull's-eye.

The sportsman who wishes to become a practical rifle shot should learn how to handle the rifle in the several useful positions, so that he may be able to sight accurately under different conditions. The off-hand position, with arm extended, is the most commonly used and best position for the sportsman to practice for use in the woods. The off-hand, with body rest, or elbow resting on the hip, is good for target shooting. The "Schuetzen" style of holding the rifle, with palm rest, is used only in fine match shooting.

The knee-rest position is often useful for the sportsman in stalking game, when it is desirable to expose oneself as little as possible. A steadier aim may be secured, especially if a strong wind is blowing. The prone position is much used by military riflemen, but they are not permitted the muzzle rest, whereas the hunter often uses it. It is easy to learn, and more accurate shooting may be done in this position than in the off-hand or knee-rest positions.

For indoor practice at a target, the .22-caliber rifle is best. By fitting up a suitable backstop, shooting may be done safely in the cellar or attic. A satisfactory backstop may be made by fastening a plate of iron into a packing box, three feet square. The plate must be set at an angle so that the bullets will be deflected to the bottom of the box.

In order that the rifleman may check up his work, it is desirable that a standard target be used. The American standard target has been adopted by practically all rifle clubs, and, as the majority of records are made upon it, the sportsman should become familiar with it. The paper targets are inexpensive, and it is easy to draw accurate homemade targets from the original. By the use of disks of black and white paper—known as gummed target pasters—one target may be used several times.

If convenient to do so, the novice should shoot a string of shots every day, in the various positions. Do not try to hurry, but shoot deliberately at first, aiming to secure a good average, rather than a few bull's-eye shots and many wild ones. With reasonable practice, it is not difficult to score eight bull's-eyes out of ten shots when using the prone position. Having attained this proficiency, the sportsman may be regarded as a fair shot, and is ready to take up outdoor target practice with the high-power rifle.

For outdoor target shooting the .22-caliber, long-rifle cartridge will give very accurate results up to 100 yards. The standard target has a bull's-eye measuring six inches in diameter for 150 yards. Shooting may be tried for a while at a fixed range, then the target may be moved to an unknown distance and angle, and the marksman can try his hand at estimating distance. Instead of changing his sights at varying distances, the sportsman should learn how to estimate the distance of the mark and the approximate elevation of the sights to land the bullet within the circle. This is valuable practice for good shooting in the woods.

After considerable practice at the stationary target, quick firing may be varied by rigging up a sliding trolley arrangement, like that shown in the page illustration. It is easily made by setting up two poles, properly braced, one about 30 feet tall, and the other about 10 feet, spaced 30 feet apart. Between the poles, about 8 feet from the ground, stretch a length of stiff telephone wire, and make a wooden target block with a metal sheave wheel, so that it may slide freely along the wire. On the tallest post, a little above the wire, fasten a metal pulley, and at the top of the pole place a sash pulley. Then attach a stout cord to the target block, reeve it through the two pulleys, and attach a sandbag, or other weight, to the end of the cord. On the shorter post, a latch, or trigger, is fastened to hold the target, which is released by pulling a string. With this easily constructed device, much valuable practice may be had, for if the pole is fairly high, the weight will cause the target to slide as rapidly as the average game bird travels. In using this moving target, just as good practice is obtained with a .22-caliber repeater as with a high-power gun. In fact, the high-velocity ammunition should be used only on a regular range, or where a suitable backstop is erected to stop the high-power bullets. Such a backstop may be constructed of heavy timber, like old railroad ties, in the form of a crib, which is filled in with sand or earth. When a natural background, such as a mound or hill, is at hand, this may be used with safety, but a rocky hillside is not satisfactory, for it is likely to deflect the bullets, and may cause injury through stray shots.

As our antlered game, like the moose, the Virginia deer, the caribou, and the elk, are held in higher esteem than other American big-game animals, a few practical hints on where to sight may serve to bring better luck to the sportsman who has yet to bring in his first head. The shoulder shot is taken by the experienced hunter whenever possible, in preference to any other. It is the object of this shot to break the shoulder joint, and thus prevent use of the forelegs. It is a vital shot, also, because there is a good chance of the bullet passing through either the heart or lungs, which will drop the game in its tracks. This is the most effective of all shots, and as the hunter more often draws a bead while the game is running away, the shoulder shot is used more than any

other. The exact spot at which the aim should be taken
depends upon the distance of the animal and its rate of movement. It is possible to land a bullet in a vital spot at distances
up to 500 yards with a high-power rifle, but it is very likely
that the game will be wounded only, and may escape to die a
lingering death. In taking long shots at big game on the run,
the sight should be taken well forward and a trifle higher
than the marks given, since the hunter must allow for the trajectory of his arm and the time the bullet takes to reach its
mark.

The front shot has as its object to hit the heart or lungs. It is
a useful shot, and the sight is taken at the cross indication on
the breast. The head shot is a brain shot, and is used only by
the experienced hunter, when it is difficult to land a shoulder
or front shot. As the brain is well up to the top of the head, the
best point of aim is midway between the eyes and a trifle
higher than their centers. This shot is most effective when the
hunter stands a trifle above the game, or shoots when the
game is charging head down. If on a level, aim just above the
eye, and if close to the game, land the bullet just below the
eye. The ear shot, as indicated by the cross, is taken at close
quarters, and the point to sight for is the inside of the ear at its
base.

A good rifle will give a lifetime of service, and the sportsman should take care of it. The best time to clean a firearm
of any kind is as soon after shooting as possible, for the
powder residue is then fresh and moist, and is more easily
and quickly removed. Black powder can be removed with a
wet rag, but smokeless powder not only leaves a little powder residue, but also a film of gummy residue on the steel
that is not apparent to the eye. Common washing soda, dissolved in water to make a saturated solution, is used to
remove it. Any of the ready-prepared nitro solvents are

good for cleaning the rifle. A good way to clean a rifle is to use strips of cotton flannel, cut into squares of such size that they will fit snugly, but may be easily pushed through the barrel on the head of the metal cleaning rod. Always clean a rifle from the breech, if possible, by resting the muzzle on a few folded papers on the floor. Push a couple of dry wipers down to the floor to remove the carbon residue. Then saturate another square of cloth with the nitro solvent, and carefully swab out the barrel, turning the rod so that it will follow the spiral rifling. Repeat the operation two or three times; then take a clean wiper, moistened with the solvent, and repeat until the barrel is well lubricated with the cleaning fluid. The barrel should be well oiled with any good, thick oil, or liquid Vaseline. The lock mechanism of the arm should be kept clean and very lightly lubricated with any good thin oil, and the gunstock polished with linseed oil.

## HOW A SHOTGUN IS MADE

Hunting and fishing have always held the most important places in the field of sport. Primitive man was an expert hunter and a skilled fisherman. He had to be in order to secure food and skins, and while but few men are now dependent upon this method of getting a living, the call of the outdoor world is still heard by millions of men and women. This, then, may be reckoned the inheritance that our primitive ancestors have bequeathed to every man, and every man will find health and recreation through it. It would be interesting to begin this chapter at the start and set down the history of weapons, trace the evolution of the hunting arm all the way from the bow down to the modern hammerless shotgun, but as this is a practical article on how to pick out a good gun and the knack of using it, only modern weapons will be discussed. The novice needs to know something of the way in which a serviceable weapon is manufactured, for with this knowledge he is better qualified to pick out a suitable arm for his own particular use.

The frame of a shotgun—that is, the part to one end of which the barrels are affixed, the stock being bolted to the other—contains the lock mechanism, and that the weapon may give the utmost satisfaction for many years, the lock must be of good quality, of the requisite temper, and the bolting mechanism—securing the barrels to the frame—must be simple, yet strong and serviceable. For the frame, a solid drop forging is milled to make a shell into which the working mechanism is fitted, and two types of frames are used in making modern shotguns. The side-plate lock is really a development of the old hammer lock, with the striker inside. This lock is preferred by some shooters because of its neat and graceful lines, and some manufacturers use this type because it enables them to make use of a lighter frame.

The box type of frame likewise has its champions and possesses certain advantages. Certainly it makes a strong and rigid frame, and for inexpensive weapons it would be difficult to improve upon. While its square, boxlike form is not graceful in line, it enables the maker to use a spiral, or coil, spring instead of a flat spring for operating the locks, which is an advantage. In brief, the merits of both types may be summed up in this fashion: The use of the box type of lock enables the maker to turn out a better quality of gun at a low price, but in the case of a well-made gun, selling for a reasonable figure, there is very little choice between them so far as dependability and long service are concerned. Both are much used by manufacturers of the finest weapons, hence the shooter may pick out the one that best suits his fancy.

## The Cocking Mechanism of the Hammerless Shotgun

The locks of the hammerless shotgun work inside of the frame or lock, and are cocked by an ingenious little mechanism operated by the movement of the barrels when they are opened. The Anson & Deely cocking mechanism is one of the oldest and best of these devices, and is still used on many American as well as European arms. The levers of this mechanism are hung with pivots in the end of the frame—one end projecting into the fore end and the opposite end resting beneath the hammer toe. As the gun is "broken," or opened, it presses down the forward end of the cocking lever, and the other end rises and pushes the hammers into the cocked position. This is the principle upon which all cocking devices are constructed, and while it works smoothly and is so simple that it is not likely to get out of order, it is mechanically weak, owing to the short frame required to secure adequate leverage. Perhaps one of the best variations of the Anson & Deely device is one employed by an American manufacturer who makes use of a rod running through the frame from the fore end to the hammer. To each end of this rod is attached a crank, so hung that as one crank is depressed the other rises and pushes the hammer to the cocked position as the barrels are swung to open the gun.

The cocking hook is an ingenious device found on American shotguns and many variations of it are, of course, used on the different makes of arms. The Parker gun is provided with a hook, working a slide, thus pulling the hammers to cock. In the Baker, a bent arm is pivoted to the breech to serve the same purpose. Another example of American ingenuity may be noted in the lug-cocking devices used on the Ithaca and Fox guns. This simple arrangement is made by connecting the toe of the hammer directly with the lug, which is an integral part of the barrel. The hammer is thus made to act as its own lever, for as the toe portion rises when the barrel is opened, the striker falls back until it is caught in the notch of the sear.

To guard against the possibility of accidental discharge of the hammerless gun, in which type of gun the hammer must be always at full cock, a safety trigger bolt is utilized. This bolt is affixed in the frame in a vertical position by pivoting it, and to the upper part of the lever is attached a slide, placed on top of the tang immediately back of the top lever which opens the barrels. As this safety slide is pushed, the lower end of the lever is brought close up against the triggers, blocking them, and thus prevents them from moving while the safety is in the "on" position. To discharge the gun, the slide must be pushed forward to the "off" position, which moves the lower end away from the triggers. This type of safety is of the nonautomatic variety and can only block the triggers when the slide is operated by the shooter.

The automatic type of safety consists of a block, or bar, fitted in the frame and extending from the safety bolt to the post of the top lever. When the top lever is pushed to one side to open the barrels, this block, or bar, pushes the safety bolt over the triggers, automatically blocking them and preventing accidental discharge. The triggers must be pressed to withdraw the automatic safety bar.

To make the shotgun less likely to go off in the hands of the careless gunner, the tumbler safety has been incorporated into the mechanism of a few American weapons. The tumbler safety is a bar, automatically operated by the triggers, and interposed between the strikers and their firing pins. This device makes it impossible for the arm to be discharged by the hammer jarring off when dropped, for the tumbler bar occupies its position between the striker and firing pins until the triggers are pulled.

The practical value of both the automatic safety and the tumbler type of bolt is questioned by practically all experienced gunners. Its presence is designed to make the arm less dangerous in the hands of careless and ignorant sportsmen. This it may serve to do, but since there should be no excuse for tolerating the latter, most handlers of the scattergun fail to see the utility of the former. The novice should lose no time in acquiring the knack of handling his chosen weapon, and if he will but exercise a little care, he will find the hand-operated safety quite sufficient, for he will not be troubled through accidental discharge of his gun. By far the larger portion of accidents occur through careless handling of the gun and by the untimely pulling of the trigger, either by dragging the gun through the brush or by nervousness, and it is impossible to make use of a safety device to prevent the accidental discharge.

## The Barrels of a Shotgun

Between fifteen and twenty years ago shotgun barrels were made by combining bars of iron and steel and welding them together to form barrels of the proper diameter or bore. When these strips of metal were twisted to make a spiral tube they were welded together to make the familiar "twist," "laminated," and "Damascus" barrels. Sometimes three, four, and five strips of iron and steel were twisted together to make the "three-stripe," "four-stripe," and "five-stripe" Damascus barrels. This old type of a barrel was strong and flexible, but being comparatively soft, it was easily damaged by denting.

The modern compressed-steel barrels are fashioned from solid drawn steel, are very hard, will stand much higher pressure than the Damascus type, and since the process of

manufacture is simpler, a first-class steel barrel may be produced at one-quarter the cost of the old type. The several
manufacturers have adopted trade names to distinguish the
various grades of steel barrels. Various trade names come
from the abroad, and those of American manufacture are
labeled "nirosteel," "armor steel," "high-pressure steel," etc.
While differences very likely exist in the quality of the different barrels sold under the several names, all the barrels
used by reputable gun builders will be found amply strong to
resist any pressure exerted by ordinary charges of powder;
hence, the cheaper guns are perfectly safe and will stand
many years of hard shooting.

## Locking the Barrels to the Frame

In the early models of the breechloader the barrels were
locked to the frame with a bolt operated by a lever placed
under the fore end. All modern guns have the top-lever
action. In this device a "lump" is fastened to the underside
of the barrels near the breech, forming a hinged joint to
which the fore end is attached when fitting the barrel and
stock together. When closed by a slide, or bolt, the breech
fits into the "lump" attached underneath the barrels.
Different makers use various forms of top-lever bolting
devices, as the "hook-rib" or "extension rib," otherwise
known as the "dolls-head," and the cross bolt first used by
Greener, the celebrated English gun builder. All of these
devices are satisfactory on a good grade of gun, but the
strongest mechanism is an American invention, known as
the Smith rotary bolt. This rotary bolt is tapered and is
pushed through an opening in the rib by means of a strong
spring. Mechanically this locking device is all that can be
desired, and it cannot loosen through manipulation,
because of its compensating feature; that is, the spring
forces the bolt farther in as the bearings become worn

through much service. Many of our well-known builders use this splendid fastening.

## Shotgun Stocks

Walnut is exclusively used for gunstocks, and the several grades are termed plain American walnut, fine American walnut, English walnut, fine English walnut, Italian walnut, and Circassian walnut. The plain American walnut is simply a common quality of black walnut, oiled and varnished, and fitted on the cheaper guns. Fine American walnut is of better grain. It is strong and durable, and when well oiled and hand-polished it makes an attractive stock for the knock-about gun. Fine English walnut is usually fitted to guns selling at a higher price, and is generally made to order. Italian walnut is a dark wood with a fine grain and is usually supplied to order on the finest wood obtainable, of a rich dark color and a fine curly grain. It is therefore expensive and only finished to order and fitted to the most expensive guns.

## The Fore End

The fore end is an extension of the stock beyond the triggers and frame and affords a grip for the extended hand, protecting it from the hot barrel-serves to lock the barrel to the frame, and likewise holds the ejector mechanism. The Deely & Edge and Snal fore ends are both used on American guns, and they are so well designed and made that it is practically impossible for the modern types to loosen even when the arm has been subjected to long, hard service. Hence this detail of the shotgun need not be considered when selecting an arm.

## Self-ejector Mechanism

Although a great many shooters do not use the self-ejector, this handy device will many times prove of great value in the field, for when the birds are coming fast and the shooter happens to score a miss, the self-ejector throws out the empty shell and enables him to shove in a fresh load to bring down the following bird. The nonejecting arm is plenty good and quick enough for trap use, for when shooting "clays," plenty of time is given each man to reload between shots, but for upland-bird and for duck shooting, the automatic ejector is a desirable addition to the double-barreled gun.

## Repeating and Automatic Shotguns

While a good double-barreled gun in the hands of the average shot will very likely bag as many birds as the shooter is entitled to—and it may be depended on to do this when fitted with a good automatic ejector—many shooters prefer the repeating gun. The hand-operated, sliding forearm, trombone-action, or pump gun is so well-known that no recommendation is needed. It will suffice to mention that it will do everything that a double-barreled gun can perform, and considering that every pump gun is self-ejecting, and its cost less than an equal grade of double gun equipped with an ejecting device, it is not difficult to understand its popularity. So far as accuracy is concerned, the repeater will shoot rather more steadily than the double-barreled gun in the hands of the average man, and after two shots have been fired, there remain four more in the magazine. Rapid firing is not always an advantage, of course, but when after ducks, the third shot is often wanted in the interval that is required to load the double-barreled gun.

The automatic, or self-loading, shotgun is the logical development of the repeater, and while its mechanism is necessarily more complicated, it has some merits peculiarly its own. The devotee of the double barrel is inclined to believe that the repeater and the automatic shotgun do not balance so well as his favorite weapon, and the man who swears by the pump gun is inclined to think that the automatic arm is balanced like a club and prone to get out of order. Both factions can put up plenty of argument to support their opinions, but to the unprejudiced gunner, both the repeater and the self-loader will prove very fine guns after the shooter has become familiar in handling them. The double-barrel is a mighty fine gun, so is the repeater and again the automatic; so let the gunner pick out the type he likes best.

## HOW TO SELECT A SHOTGUN

That the shooter may not be handicapped by using a misfit gun, it is well to make a selection at one of the larger dealers where guns of various sizes, weights, and lengths, as well as drops in stocks, may be tried until one is found that fits the gunner the best. A good shot can pick up almost any gun and do fairly accurate shooting with it, but he can do better work with a gun fitting him properly. The chief measurements of a gunstock are the length and drop of the stock, and the drop and shape of the comb. The ordinary thickness of the grip will suit the average hand, but in the case of unusually large or small hands, this must be taken into consideration. For the average man these measurements will probably be about right: Length of stock, from forward trigger to center of butt plate, 14 to 14½ inches, drop at comb, 1½ to 1⅞ inches, which will give corresponding drop at the heel, from 2½ to 3 inches. A fairly straight stock of good length may be reckoned an advantage for trapshooting, but for use in the field, a somewhat crooked stock with more drop at the comb, say, 1 ⅝ inches with 2⅜-inch drop at the heel will more fully meet the average shooter's idea of a well-balanced gun. However, as men differ, and there are men, every shooter must decide this question for himself. So far as the circumference of the grip is concerned, the size of the shooter's hand and the length of his fingers will decide this detail. For a small hand, a 7-inch grip is about right, while a grip of 7½ inches will probably fit the large hand well. The question of straight or pistol grip is purely a matter of personal taste, for one is as good as the other so far as accurate handling of the gun is concerned.

## The Gauge, or Size of Bore

The 10-gauge may be occasionally useful for long-range duck and goose shooting, but for ordinary duck and upland use the 12-gauge is plenty large enough. The larger the gauge the greater will be the killing zone, and up to their ranges the small bores may, for all practical purposes, be regarded as shooting quite as accurately and with as much power as the heavier gauges; that is, the small bores will shoot to kill if held correctly. The standard 12-gauge gun is fitted with 30-inch barrels, weighs 7 to 8 pounds, and the standard load for the field is 3 drams of powder and 1⅛ ounces of shot. This gives a killing range up to 40 yards. The standard 16-gauge, with 30-inch barrels, weighs from 6½ to 7¼ pounds, and the standard load is 2½ drams of powder and 1 ounce of shot, with a killing range up to 35 yards. The standard 20-gauge, with 28-inch barrels, weighs from 5 to 6½ pounds and the standard load is 2¼ drams of powder and ⅞ ounce of shot. Best killing range up to 30 yards.

For an all-purpose gun, suitable for wild fowling as well as upland shooting, the 12-gauge is the best choice, although the 16-gauge will be found a hard-hitting weapon. For the good shot, the 20-gauge will prove a fine little arm for upland work, only the gunner must shoot well with the small bore to kill his bird clean. Contrary to the notion, the large bore, not the small gauge, will bring the most game to the novice's bag.

## The Choke and Pattern of a Gun

Having picked out a gun that "fits the man," the matter of

choke and pattern should be considered. For trapshooting and for wild fowling, the full-choke gun may be considered a necessity, since it will throw the charge of shot within a relatively small circle; in other words, make a denser pattern. Choke-boring is accomplished by constricting the barrel at the muzzle from 1½₅ to ⅟₅₀ inch, the amount of taper, depending on the size of the bore and gauge. The narrowing of the muzzle forces the charge of shot together and prevents the pellets from scattering over a wide area. Guns are bored with varying degrees of choke, from the full to the plain cylinder, and the manufacturers compare them by recording the number of pellets that any given choke will shoot in a 30-inch circle at 30 yards, or any other range selected as the maximum distance. This gives the pattern from which we find that the full choke produces 70 percent, the half choke 50 percent, and the cylinder 30 percent.

For trapshooting and wild fowling the expert considers it essential that his 12-gauge should be capable of throwing not less than 300 pellets; hence he selects a full-choked gun with a pattern of 300 or better. As a full-choked 16-gauge will pattern about 275, it may be used for ducks with good success. For a general-purpose gun, a pattern from 250 to 275 will prove quite satisfactory for ducks and upland game, and this may be had by picking out a half-choked 12-gauge, or selecting a full-choked 16-gauge. The 20-gauge gives a pattern of about 245 shot, and thus scatters its charge over too large a circle to prove effective on wild fowl, although it is very effective on upland game, which is flushed not over 35 yards from the shooter. A gun patterning from 225 to 250 may be considered the ideal upland gun, and this may be had by choosing a quarter-choked 12-gauge, a half-choked 16-gauge, or a full-choked 20-gauge gun. These are known as "open-choked" guns, are the most effective at short ranges, up to 35 yards, and cannot be depended upon to kill clean when used at longer ranges.

## HOW TO SHOOT WITH BOTH EYES OPEN

To handle the weapon well is the desire of every sportsman, and this knack is not difficult to attain, providing the novice will make a good beginning. First of all, it is necessary to hold the gun correctly, and while the forward hand may grip the fore end at any convenient point, a well-extended arm gives a better control of the gun when aiming, by giving free play to all the muscles of the arm; hence the gun should be held in a manner natural to the shooter, rather than in imitation of the style of another.

The old manner of aiming the shotgun by closing one eye and sighting along the rib is fast becoming obsolete, for better shooting may be done by keeping both eyes open. Doctor Carter was the first great exponent of binocular shooting, and while but few men can hope to approach this famous gunner's skill, everyone can learn to handle a shotgun more quickly and with greater accuracy by following his common-sense method. It may appear a bit strange at first to disregard the sights and keep both eyes open, and aim the gun by merely pointing it in the desired direction, but to sight along the rib and attempt to see the bead on the muzzle end can only make a slow and poky shot. This old-fashioned method may be good enough for making patterns on a stationary target, but it is not much of a success for wing shooting. For fine rifle shooting the left eye is invariably closed for target work, but for snap-shooting both eyes are kept open, the sights are disregarded, and the aim is taken by pointing the gun at the object to be hit. Of course, there are many good gunners who shoot with one eye closed, but the novice who is anxious to become a good wing shot should make it a point to practice with both eyes open. Vision is always clearer, and the objects more accurately judged with both eyes open than with one, and when this is done, and one eye controls the line of aim, the shooter is not so likely to make mistakes in estimating the distances and the rapidity of the flight of his game. In shooting, the right eye naturally governs the right shoulder, and vice versa, and this is so because habit has trained the eye to do this. To find which is the master eye, hold a pencil out at arm's length and point it at some small distant object with both eyes open, then close the left eye, and if the pencil still points to the object, the right eye controls the vision, and is the master eye. Should the closing of the left eye alter the aim, the right eye must be trained by practice until it becomes the master eye, or else the gun must be shot from the left shoulder, which is many times more difficult. The modern way of mastering wing shooting is to point the gun where both eyes are looking, and after a little practice this may be done quickly, and the charge thrown more accurately at the object than by closing one eye, or sighting along the barrel in the old manner.

## THE KNACK OF HITTING A FLYING TARGET

When shooting at clay targets, or at a flying bird, allowance must be made for the swiftness of flight and the distance from the shooter to the game, or in other words the shooter must calculate the speed of the flying target, the gun may be directly thrown at the mark and discharged as quickly as possible, or the gun may cover the mark and be quickly swung ahead and the charge sent at the point where the swiftly moving bird will be found when the shot gets there. Snap-shooting is only possible when the birds are flying straight away or quartering, and as the shooter fires point-blank at the rapidly moving bird, the shot must be delivered so rapidly that only a very quick and responsive trigger and a fast man back of it can hope to score even a fair percentage of hits. A more certain way of aiming a snap shot is to throw the shot at the point where the line of the aim and the flight of the bird intersect. For shots at quail, woodcock, and partridge in the brush, the quick snap shot often must be taken, regardless of the chances of missing, for to delay even a second will lose the bird. When a bird rises near the shooter, no allowance of lead or elevation are required, and the charge is thrown directly at the bird.

The rapid swing, however, is the most accurate manner of using the shotgun, at all angles and at any distance within the killing zone of the weapon. To make this shot, the gun must be thrown up behind the bird and then rapidly swung ahead of it, throwing the charge without checking the swing of the arm. In this style of snap-shooting, the elevation of the gun must be identical with the flight of the bird, inasmuch as the gun follows it, and if the gun is swung about three times as fast as the bird is traveling, plenty of allowance for the time necessary to press the trigger and deliver the shot at the determined point will be made.

To swing deliberately and cover the bird with the sight, then shove the gun ahead to fire the proper lead, is all right for duck shooting where the game is usually seen approaching and thus remains within range for a longer time. But this deliberate style of handling the gun is far too slow for the uplands, and since the rapid swing is the only accurate manner of cutting down the fast bird, and usually useful for wild fowling, the novice should confine his practice to this practical style of wing shooting.

### Stationary-Target Practice

The first great mistake the novice is likely to make is the natural one of supposing that he must take his gun to the field and learn how to handle it by practicing at flying game. This is by no means the best method, and there is scarcely a poorer way of becoming a wing shot, because the gunner is intent upon bagging the game and forgets to observe the many little points of gunnery, shooting high and low, and making the hundred and one mistakes of judgment he would not be guilty of when practicing at a stationary mark. Snap- and wing shooting is the last word in shotgun handling, requiring quickness in throwing the gun, as well as a trained eye to calculate the distance from and the speed of the flying target. To acquire confidence in using the gun, begin by shooting at a fixed mark. A good target may be made by obtaining a dozen, or two, sheets of stout wrapping paper and painting a four-inch circle in the center of each sheet. Tack it up on a board fence, or on a board hung on a tree, measure off sixty feet, and try a shot. The shot will not spread very much at this range, and it will be an easy matter to determine the result of your skill in holding a dead-on to the large mark. To avoid flinching and other movements of the head and body, caused by the recoil, begin your first practicing with a light powder-and-shot charge, say, about 2 drams of bulk measure, or its equivalent in smokeless, and ⅞ ounces of No. 8 or 9 shot. There is no advantage in using a heavier charge, and the recoil of the gun will appear much greater in deliberate shooting at a target than is likely to be felt during the excitement incidental to shooting in the field. A dozen shots at these targets will enable the gunner to make a good score by deliberate holding, and when this can be done, without flinching, snap- and wing shooting may begin.

## Snap- and Wing Shooting

The object which the gunner should now strive for is to train the eye, hand, and gun to work in unison, and to do this, bring the gun quickly to the shoulder, point it to the mark, and press the trigger without stopping the upward and even swing of the barrels. At the first few trials some difficulty may be encountered with the pressing of the trigger at the proper moment, but a little practice will soon tell how to time the shots. Note the phrase, "press the trigger," for the trigger is not pulled by the forefinger alone, but rather pressed by closing both hands, the forward hand on the fore end pushing and closing, and the hand grasping the stock being drawn back and squeezed at the same instant. This is easily done, but rather hard to picture. After a few trials with an empty gun, the novice will see the point, and also discover the fact that the recoil of the arm is much lessened by this proper grip of the weapon.

Confine the first practice in snap-shooting to throwing the gun to the shoulder, and when proficient in hitting the mark, try a snap shot by swinging the gun from the side, right to left and also left to right. Do not attempt to check the even swing of the gun, but rather let the barrels swing past the mark, concentrating the mind upon pressing the trigger the instant the line of aim covers the mark. Practice swinging slowly, and after being able to hit the mark with the center of the charge pretty regularly, increase the speed of the swing. In doing this it will be discovered that the speed of pressing the trigger must also be increased to balance the speed of the moving barrel, and very likely it will be found that the natural tendency is to press the trigger a bit late. This is the common mistake that practically every novice makes when in the field, although the error is likely to pass unnoticed when after game.

As the gunner acquires proficiency in swinging the gun from side to side, try swinging the gun at different angles, changing the angle of the swing with each shot, from right to left and upward, at an oblique angle upward, and so on, until it is possible to hit the mark with a fair certainty from a variety of angles. When trying out the several swings, one should always begin slowly and increase the speed of the swing as he becomes more expert, only making sure to shoot by calculation and not by guess. The manner of acquiring expertness sounds easy and is comparatively easy, and, as it is the backbone of snap-shooting, improvement will be rapid if the novice is willing to practice slowly and master each detail in turn. Do not make the mistake of overdoing the thing at the outset by shooting too long at a time. A box of twenty-five loads is ample for a day's practice, since it is not how much one shoots, but how well, that counts.

## Value of the Second Barrel in Shooting

The use of the second barrel should not be overlooked in practicing with the idea of becoming an all-around wing shot, for the second shot is often needed to kill a cripple, or bring down a bird that has been missed with the first shot. Two-shot practice should begin by placing two paper targets about twenty feet apart, then shooting at the first one and continuing to swing the gun to cover the second target. Practice swinging from various angles as directed for the initial practice, increasing the speed of the swing as proficiency is gained, and fail not to profit by the mistakes which must inevitably occur to all who try to master the shotgun. After a reasonable amount of practice, conducted along these lines, the gunner may venture afield, and if his acquaintance includes an old seasoned sportsman who will point out the mistakes made, much may be learned regarding the knack of handling the gun, as well as relating to the haunts and habits of our wild game birds.

### Snap-Shooting at Moving Targets

When the gunner has reached the point where he can hit the stationary target by swinging his gun both fast and slow, he has acquired better control of the weapon than many old shooters, and he is well prepared to take up snap-shooting at flying or moving targets. The access to a gun club where clay birds may be shot at will prove of much value, but this is not absolutely necessary, since tin cans, bits of brick, and bottles, thrown in the air at unknown angles by a companion, will afford the needed variety. Better than this is one of the inexpensive "hand traps" which project the regulation clay targets by means of a powerful spring worked by a trigger. One of the large powder manufacturers makes a trap of this kind, and a very good trap can be had for $1.50. The standard clay targets cost about $2.50 a barrel of 500. Practice of this sort may be made a very interesting and highly instructive sport, providing the unexpected angles, thus simulating the many-angled flight of the live bird.

## CLEANING AND CARE OF THE GUN

A good shotgun is a thoroughly reliable and dependable weapon, but as with all tools of the sportsman's craft, the best results can only be had when the arm is in good condition. It is gun wisdom always to clean the weapon after a day's shooting, and the amateur should make it a positive rule never to put his handgun away until it is cleaned. The sooner firearms are cleaned after the firing the better, and if cleaned before the burnt powder has had time to corrode the steel, much future trouble is saved. In cleaning the barrels, never rest the muzzle against the floor. If a rest is needed, use an old piece of carpet or a bundle of rags. Clean from the breech end only, as any slight dust, or burr, at the muzzle will greatly impair the shooting qualities of any firearm. Never use a wire-wheel scratch brush, as it will scratch the polished steel; a soft brass wire cleaner is the only suitable implement for this work. There are several good cleaners to be had. For removing any rust deposits, a brass brush may be used, while for ordinary cleaning, plenty of cloth should be run through the barrels, taking care that it touches every part of the interior. This is easily done by rotating the cleaning rod as it is pushed through the barrel from the breech to the muzzle. When putting the gun away, the barrels should be stopped, at the breech and muzzle, with tightly fitting cords, or gun ropes may be run through the barrels after soaking them in some good oil. To prevent rusting, cover the metal, outside as well as inside the barrels, by smearing on a little heavy lubricating oil. Slipcovers of chamois are often used to protect the stock and barrels before putting them in the leather case, but stout woolen covers are better, since chamois is likely to absorb more or less moisture.

The mechanism of a gun is not exactly complicated, but the novice had better leave well enough alone and not attempt to dismount the locks or tinker with the mechanism. The modern steel barrel is very hard and not easily dented, but if so injured, it's better to ship it to the factory for repairs than to trust it to the crude methods of the average gun repairman.

A gun should be given ordinary good care, and this is not forthcoming if one makes a practice of opening it and letting the barrels drop down with a bang. Snapping the triggers on an empty barrel is likewise foolish. If one desires to practice trigger pressing, put a couple of empty shells in the barrels.

If one owns a good-grade shotgun, the stock is probably finished in oil and hand-rubbed to a nice, durable polish. On cheap arms the varnish is usually employed to give an attractive finish in the store. Of course, this varnish will scratch, and otherwise come off, and spoil the appearance of the arm. If a good finish is wanted, do not revarnish the stock, but remove all the old varnish by using a little varnish remover, and rub down with oil. For an extrafine polish, wet the wood to raise the grain; rub down with very fine sandpaper; wet the wood again, and sandpaper a second or a third time; then rub down with oil until the wood is saturated with it, and polish with a cloth, using plenty of pressure, and the stock will be as fine in appearance as if it had the "London oil finish" supplied with all high-grade guns.

—Stillman Taylor

## MISCELLANEOUS POWDER FLASHES

**Hints to Amateurs**—Use care in filling shells. To obtain uniform loads powder and shot should be accurately measured; try and get them all alike. Don't break the grains by pounding the powder (*and never compress nitro powders*).

**For Trapshooting**—At inanimate targets the following is a popular load for a 10-gauge gun: 4 drams *Hazard's Trap Powder No. 2*; two No. 9 and one No. 10 black edge wad (split) in order named; 1¼ ounces (dipped measure) chilled shot No. 8; one-half of a No. 10 black edge (split) or shot shell crimped. Many shooters prefer 3¾ drams of powder, and this quantity of Trap No. 2 is sufficient. It is desirable to have a light paper wad next to powder to prevent the grease from wads affecting it.

**Charges for Breechloaders**—For guns under 8 pounds in weight, 12 bore, 3 to 3½ drams *Hazard Powder*, 1⅛ ounces shot; 10 bore, 3¼ to 4 drams powder, 1¼ ounces shot.

**Exact Amounts**—To give satisfactory results can only be determined by repeated trials—guns like shooters vary. The distribution of shot can be increased either by decreasing the quantity of powder or increasing the charge of shot. To produce better penetration, increase the powder, decrease the shot.

**Hazard's Trap Powder**—No. 1 (fine), No. 2 (medium), No. 3 (course). No. 2 is popular for both trap and field shooting, being slightly quicker than F.F.G. Kentucky.

**Duck Shooting Powder**—No. 1 fine to No. 6 coarse; finer size for field shooting, the coarser for water fowl.

**Look Out for Accidents**—Never compress *nitro* powders. Black powders require compression, but to do this on nitro powders might lead to serious results (a funeral perhaps).

Advice for use of smokeless powder:

**Shells**—Use shells adapted to bulk smokeless powder.

**Powder**—The best loads for a 12-gauge gun are 2¾, 3, and 3¼ drams, standard measure filled and struck. The smaller loads give slight recoil, high velocity, and very close pattern, and are well adapted to general shooting. For a quick, far-reaching load 3¼ drams is recommended. With this charge a close pattern is maintained and the necessary lead on quartering birds greatly reduced.

**Wads**—In general, one trap or field wad, two or three black edge wads, and a thin cardboard wad over the shot will give excellent results. One cardboard, one white felt, with black edge wads to fill, will be found equally satisfactory for use over the powder. Wadding ought to be chosen of a thickness that will leave from a 1/4 to 3/8 inch for a tight crimp and the wads should be seated firmly on the powder charge.

10-gauge guns, 3 to 4 drams and 1¼ ounce shot.
12-gauge guns, 2¾ to 3¼ drams and 1, 1⅛, or 1¼ ounce shot.

*Proper loads of these powders are:*

20-gauge guns, 2 to 2½ drams by measure.
16-gauge guns, ¼ to 2¼ drams by measure.
12-gauge guns, 2¾ to 3½ drams by measure.
10-gauge guns, 3½ to 4½ drams by measure.
8-gauge guns, 4½ to 6¾ drams by measure.

Always use paper shells adapted to bulk nitro powders, and place enough tight-fitting wads over powder, firmly pressed down, to leave about 1/4 inch of paper for a solid crimp.

## The Perfect and Imperfect Crimp

E—The imperfect crimp.    C—The square crimp.    D—The round crimp.
C and D are correct crimps.

**Loads for Rifle Powders**—(Dupont Smokeless No. 1) 45, 70, 405, 28 grains; 38, 70, 255, 25 grains; for high-power rifle use 30-caliber annular smokeless rifle powder; 303 Savage, 29 grains; 30–30 Winchester or Marlin, 26½-grains.

**Laflin & Rand**—(Lightning Smokeless) 30–30 Winchester, 23 grains or 1⅛ drams; 303 Savage, 27 grains or 1¼ drams; 303 British, 28 grains or 1⁵⁄₁₆ drams.

**Walsrode High-Pressure Rifle Powder**—30–30 or 303 Savage, 25 grains.

## Two Good Loads for Trap Work

No. 1—3 drams Hazard Smokeless. 1 No. 12 trap or field. 1 No. 12 white felt, ⅜-inch. 1 No. 12 black edge, ⅛ inch. 1¼ ounces No. 7½ chilled shot. Space for good crimp.

No. 2—3 drams Hazard Smokeless. 1 No. 12 card. 2 No. 12 black edge, ¼ inch. 1 No. 12 black edge, ⅛ inch. 1⅛ ounces No. 7½ chilled shot. Space for good crimp.

Still another one—3 drams Hazard Smokeless. 1 No. 12 top shot wad. 3 No. 12 pink edge, ¼ inch. 1⅛ ounces No. 7½ chilled shot. Space for good crimp.

## Hints for Shotgun Shooters

**The Best Boat for Duck Hunting**—A scull boat with cockpit. The Mullins duck boat (steel) painted dead grass color. *(See Boats.)*

**Best Dog for Duck Hunters**—Cross between a Newfoundland and setter, or a retriever and water spaniel, or a cross between the setter and spaniel; best color, liver color.

**Best Blinds for Duck Hunting**—The natural grass or rushes that abound in the vicinity; use plenty of them.

**The Best Rifle for Small Game**—Or for target practice is of course largely a matter of choice. Either the Stevens, Remington or Winchester are accurate guns. A good choice is the Winchester 25020, either single shot or half-magazine repeater, equipped with Lyman combination rear sight: Lyman leaf in lieu of the regular rear sight on the barrel and Lyman ivory bead foresight. It is satisfactory for either smokeless or black powders.

**The Best Ammunition**—For rifles is that made by Union Metal Cartridge Co., or Winchester Repeating Arms Co.

**The Best Shotgun**—Is hard to determine, there are many good ones. The Greener being a splendid weapon; following close comes the L. C. Smith, Parker, Ithaca (American make).

**When Using a High-Power Rifle**—Fit to the butt of it a good recoil pad, and have your rifle fitted with a Lyman leaf sight; fold down the crotch, raise the bar, and use the ivory bead for front; these are better for shooting trim than any globe peep or crotch sights, which are good for target uses but not for killing game.

**The Best Repeating Shotgun**—The Winchester shotgun is probably the best of its kind; its action is reasonably smooth and reliable. It can be used as a large ball gun, and if properly loaded ammunition is used, is a most satisfactory arm.

**Try Using the Right Barrel**—For objects passing to the left, left barrel for those to the right on long ranges.

**A Wire Scratch Brush**—Will not scratch the interior of barrels and is invaluable for cleaning a shotgun. Rust can be removed by a rag dipped in kerosene if not pitted in. Wipe well dry and oil afterward or Vaseline.

**Gun for Brush Shooting**—Right barrel cylinder, left modified choke bored. For field shooting right barrel modified, left full choke. Trap shooting both barrels full choked or first barrel modified choke.

**Don't Change**—Your gun or rifle if it is a good one. Stick to it. Change your methods, which are most apt to be at fault if fault exists.

**Choke Bore Guns**—Ensure close shooting and good penetration. For shooting at close range a cylinder bore is preferable. Such a gun will shoot spherical bullets up to fifty yards.

**Auxiliary Rifle Barrels**—Can be placed in temporarily and used in the barrel of a shotgun of 10 or 12 bore.

**Chilled Shot**—Is better than soft shot in many respects.

**To Scatter Shot**—Place one wad on the powder, two wads between the shot, over the whole put a thick wad. Never use poor homemade wads.

**Quick Shooting**—Is essential when using a shotgun. Shoot the instant your gun points as closely as possible without taking second aim.

### Velocity of Shot from a 12-Gauge Gun

| Powder | Drams | Size of Shot | Ounces | Range in Feet | Mean Velocity in Feet per Second |
|--------|-------|--------------|--------|---------------|----------------------------------|
| H | 2½ | 2 | 1¼ | 50 | 1,018 |
| H | 2½ | 2 | 1¼ | 100 | 865 |
| H | 2½ | 2 | 2¼ | 100 | 854 |
| D | 3 | 7 | 1⅛ | 100 | 776 |
| D | 3 | 7 | 1¼ | 100 | 783 |
| D | 3 | 7 | 1¼ | 50 | 855 |
| H | 2½ | 2 | 1¼ | 50 | 995 |

**Plant Wild Rice**—If the sportsmen will do this in the fall of the year, he will be amply repaid for his pains later. Ducks will not linger in waters devoid of food. It is to your interest to plant wild rice.

**For Duck Shooting**—Use a 10-bore shotgun, 8½ to 9½ pounds, full choke, of a 12-gauge. Best time October and November.

**To Scull a Boat**—With one oar, place oar over the stern or rear of boat in a rowlock secured there for the purpose, and thrusting the blade in the water deeply, move it so as to describe as near as possible a series of turns similar to the capital letter L, allowing the blade of the oar to take as large a figure as possible but restricting the movement of your hands to as small a figure as you can. To get the idea better, take a pencil and write a series of capital *L*s in quick succession one under the other without stopping—try it. I have taught a dozen duck hunters the idea by this simple plan.

**Decoy Duck Hunting**—Try a small-bore rifle for out-of-range birds, cripples, stragglers, etc.

**If Ducks Alight**—Out of range of your decoys, disperse them lest they attract others from your decoys—go after them.

**Ducks Approaching Decoys**—And flying with the wind invariably pass over the decoys, then swing around to alight.

**Try Trolling**—For canvas back or broad bills especially.

**Best Time for Duck Shooting**—Just before daylight or before dark.

**A Slight Noise**—Or whistle will often cause ducks to group or close together.

**For Wild Geese**—Use a 10-bore gun, 4½ drams powder, 1¼ to 1½ ounces No. 2 shot. Best time is in snowstorm as they are then bewildered and restless; mallards also are similarly affected.

**If at Forty Yards**—A foot seems too far ahead, make it two, keep the gun moving and the bird falls dead.

**Choosing a Shotgun for the Condition**—Use a cylinder bore for brush shooting; a modified choke for field use; full choke for wild fowl; or a combination of two of the three; let the barrels be 30 or 32 inch, with the gun weighing about 7 pounds. For duck shooting both barrels full choke is best.

**Shot Falling**—A charge of shot will fall 8 inches in 40 to 50 yards.

**Shooting at Close Range**—The cylinder-bored shotgun is perfect.

**To Test the Fit of a Shotgun**—Bring it to the shoulder; if you do not have to crane or stretch the neck to sight along the barrels, it is a good fit.

**Shooting Spherical Bullets**—Use the cylinder bore so as the ball will pass through the barrel easily; it will carry accurately up to 50 yards with force.

**To Scatter Shot**—Place one wad on the powder, two or three between the shot, and use thin wads; over the whole put a thick wad.

**Shell Extractors**—Always carry in a handy pocket a good shell extractor. It is well worth its cost and more.

**Reloading Shells**—Good paper shells (not abused) can be reloaded six or more times with safety.

**In Shooting Flying Birds**—The aim should be from a few inches to a few feet in advance of the bird, according to distance, speed, etc.; from three inches to even three feet or more at times.

**Don't Shoot**—At an incoming bird; wait until it passes you.

**A Leather Coat**—Should be used for fall or cold-weather duck shooting; if too heavy, choose the yellow oilskin or waterproof canvas if wet weather especially.

**"Trolling for Ducks"**—Attract their attention by waving a red bandanna handkerchief on a stick, keeping yourself out of sight; ducks are inquisitive and will often swim up to investigate, unless they are very wild.

**Best Boat for Duck Hunting**—Mullin's duck boat. Scull oar rigged with cockpit covered with brush and hay or rushes as a blind.

**Duck Shooters**—With a rubber blanket and air cushion can sit or lay on wet ground or marsh all day.

**Best Shells to Reload**—For shotguns Winchester, Yellow Rival, N.M.C., Nitro Club, New Victor, Peter's, etc.

**Use a Cylinder Bore**—If you desire to use *round ball or bullet* good for 50 to 75 yards; large game shooting, use a patched ball (to gauge the size of your gun), load 4 to 4½ drams powder, F.F.G.; ⅜ felt pad on powder, ball seated *snugly* on top of wad, a little lubricant put around it and a wad of shell as in gallery ammunition.

**Twist of Rifle Barrels**—A proper twist is one that will spin a bullet fast enough to keep it *point on* to the limit of its range or flight, thus assuring accuracy. If the twist is too slow, the flight of bullets will be untrue and it will "tumble and keyhole," passing through the air longways instead of point on as it should. On the other hand, if the twist is too quick the bullet will *spin too rapidly,* rending its flight unsteady, causing it to wobble, spin, and hum like a top.

**Incoming Birds**—Swing well ahead, keep your gun moving with the bird, pulling the trigger the instant the bird reaches the sight of your barrels.

**Side Shots**—Aim and swing with the bird and well ahead, according to distance, wind, etc., hold well ahead, so as the shot will have time to reach him.

**Birds Alighting**—Or descending, hold well under, always ahead of them, so as they will not fly with the shot.

**Duck Hunting**—In boats, leave the dog home, unless your clothes are waterproof and you don't mind his shaking the water off when he returns to boat. Making a blind decoy out of your boat is better, and use decoys.

**Always Steer Clear of Fences**—They scare any birds, ducks especially.

**In Stormy Weather**—Seek for ducks in heavy timbered woods or sheltered places.

**In Cleaning Guns**—Nothing excels kerosene or benzine, afterward wiped and rubbed well with clean, dry rags (and elbow grease), then moistened with a little Vaseline.

**Secret of Becoming a Good Shoot**—First, correctly judging distance. Second, speed of object (if moving) fired at. Third, holding the gun so as the object will meet the shot or bullet at the same time the bullet reaches it. Nine out of ten make the serious mistake of shooting behind. Fourth, making allowances for wind drift of shot correctly. Sixth, closely observing the faults of every shot and rectifying the errors.

**For Duck Shooting**—Use Nos. 5-6-7-8 chilled shot, as some guns throw certain shot better than others. See which your gun is best suited for.

**Use Waterproof Shells (Paper)**—For duck hunting, and never go on a trip without decoys; assorted ones. Don't select all one kind. Don't forget the Allen duck call, and to use the ducks you shot as additional decoys, the more the better.

**Best Dog for Duck Hunting**—A good retriever, water spaniel, or a cross between a spaniel or setter.

**To Imitate a Duck Quack**—Press the tip of your tongue at the upper roof of your mouth near the upper teeth and say "quack"; or say "me-amph" loud; geese, "ah-hunk."

**Use Dead Ducks**—As decoys (all you have), stiffening their heads with a wooden skewer.

**Best Time for Duck Hunting**—November and December. Best gun: full choke or right barrel modified choke; left, full choke, 10-gauge.

**Shot for Birds**—Prairie chicken, Nos. 6–7; quail, No. 8; teal duck, Nos. 7–8; mallards, 5–6–7; swan, Nos. 1–2; geese, Nos. 1–2–3; blue bill, No. 6–7; canvasback, No. 4–5; gray and widgeon, Nos. 5–7; redheads, No. 6; pintails, Nos. 5–6; grouse, Nos. 6–7; snipe, Nos. 8–9.

**Duck Shooter's Outfit**—Clothes dead grass color, rubber coat dead grass color, long rubber boots, wristlets and gloves.

## Table of Charges for a 12-Gauge Gun

| | | | | |
|---|---|---|---|---|
| Woodcock | 3¼ drs. | 1 oz. | No. 10 | 510 |
| Snipe | 3¼ drs. | 1⅛ oz. | No. 9 | 405 |
| Quail and plover | 3½ drs. | 1⅛ oz. | No. 9 | 395 |
| Prairie chicken (Aug.-Sept.) | 3½ drs. | 1⅛ oz. | No. 7 | 220 |
| Prairie chicken (Oct.-Nov.-Dec.) | 4 drs. | 1⅛ oz. | No. 6 | 158 |
| Ruffed grouse | 3½ drs. | 1⅛ oz. | No. 8 | 300 |
| Squirrels and rabbits | 3½ drs. | 1⅛ oz. | No. 6 | 160 |
| Teals, pintails, etc. | 3¾ drs. | 1⅛ oz. | No. 7 | 218 |
| Mallards, canvasbacks, etc. | 4 drs. | 1⅛ oz. | No. 5 | 115 |
| Geese and brant | 4 drs. | 1 oz. | No. 1 | 45 |
| Turkeys | 4 drs. | 1⅛ oz. | No. 4 | 95 |
| Deer (cylinder bore only) | 4 drs. | 3 layers of buckshot | | |

# SPEED OF BIRDS' FLIGHT

The highest speed of flight in miles per hour in full plumage is estimated as follows:

Crow, 25 to 40 miles
Mallard, black duck, and shoveler, 40 to 50
Pintail, 50 to 60
Wood duck, 55 to 60
Pigeon and gadwall, 60 to 70
Redhead, 80 to 90
Blue-winged and red-tailed teal, 80 to 100
Bluebill, 80 to 110
Canvasback, 80 to 120
Sparrow, 40 to 92
Hawk, 40 to 150
Wild geese, 80 to 90

The distance traveled by birds in ⅛ second is as follows:

At a rate of 5 miles per hour, .92 feet
Rate of 10 miles per hour, 1.83 feet

Rate of 12 miles, 2.2 feet
20 miles, 3.66 feet
30 miles, 5.5 feet
40 miles, 7.33 feet
60 miles, 11 feet
80 miles, 14.66 feet
90 miles, 16.05 feet
100 miles, 18.33 feet
120 miles, 22 feet
150 miles, 27.5 feet

**In Estimating Distances**—Underestimating is most common; it is rare that overestimating distance occurs.

**Never Use**—A cartridge or rifle of over .45-caliber or a bullet over 405 grains in weight.

**Always Follow**—Powder makers' advice in loading cartridges. Don't experiment, this is for experts, not for you to do.

**Best Powder for Shotgun Cartridges**—Hazards Electric, Dupont's Diamond Grain, Shultze, King's, etc.

**A Leaded Rifle Barrel**—Renders the arm useless for accuracy.

**A Lubricator Receipt**—Pure fresh beef tallow and Vaseline to soften it is as good as the best.

**Powder Is Bought**—By avoirdupois weight, but in weighing it for rifles the apothecaries' weight is used. Avoirdupois weight is 16 drams equal 1 ounce, 16 ounces equal 1 pound. Apothecaries, 20 grains equal 1 scruple, 3 scruples equal 1 dram, 8 drams equal 1 ounce, 12 ounces 1 pound.

**Always Use**—Soft pointed bullets for game hunting. They kill cleanly and quickly.

**Choice of a Rifle**—A .303-caliber magazine rifle or .35 caliber is best for general purposes. As to length of barrel, the longer barrel will do more accurate shooting. But for hunting where shooting is seldom done at over 250 yards the difference is hardly appreciable, provided the barrel is sufficient length to permit a nearly complete combustion of the powder. *(See About Rifles.)*

**Express Bullets**—Are always superior to solid bullets for hunting purposes. They are sure killers for deer, elk, moose, and similar game. They mushroom on impact or spread, tearing open a large wound and killing quickly, much more so than the regular pencil size and pointed hard bullet.

**The All-Round Shotgun**—A 12-gauge gun, weight about 7 pounds, 30-inch barrels, right barrel cylinder or modified choke, left barrel for full choke.

**A Rubber Recoil Pad**—Is an excellent device, if your gun kicks or affects your shooting.

**Use a Glove Finger**—On your trigger finger if it becomes sore or tender.

**A Good Load for 12-Bore Gun**—3 to 3½ drams of powder, 1⅛ ounces of No. 6 shot.

**Never Use Cheap Ammunition**—Buy the very best from most reliable dealers.

**Never Make Your Own Wads**—If you want to be sure of satisfactory results in shooting.

**What Gunpowder Is**—Saltpeter, 75 percent; charcoal, 15 percent; sulfur, 10 percent.

**The Ivory Bead Shotgun Sight**—Is an excellent one.

**You Can Obtain**—A supplementary chamber which can be placed in the chamber of your hunting rifle, so as to shoot therefrom pistol cartridges for practice or small game (called rifle cartridge bushings) chambered for .32-caliber Smith & Wesson or Colt's new police center fire cartridges, which admits of the regular short or long being used in .303-caliber rifles, all .30-caliber or Winchester .32 special for short-range work or killing small game. Or you can obtain miniature cartridges for small-game shooting.

**The Ideal Combined Holster**—And carbine stock attached to a modern pistol converts it into a rifle. An absolutely unique article for sportsmen, travelers, prospectors, cattlemen, officers, and all who use large-caliber weapons. Transforms a revolver or pistol into a rifle instantaneously. Makes every person a good revolver shot, ensuring absolute accuracy of aim. Attaches by removing plates from grip and substituting special plates furnished. No mutilation of weapon. Holster feature absolutely original—weapon cannot be shaken out or dropped out. Holsters now ready for Smith & Wesson .38 Military; Colt's New Army and New Navy and Luger Automatic Pistol.

**A Practical Rifle from a Shotgun**—Can be made by using the Elterich Rifle Bullet Shell, converting a 12-gauge gun into a rifle using 32–20 and 32 S.& W. calibers. (Made for 10-, 12-, or 16-gauge shotguns.) This rifled shell is not an auxiliary barrel, but is actually a shell made of brass and so constructed that it will fit into any 12-gauge shotgun. Into this shell is fitted a rifled steel barrel, chambered for bullet cartridges. The outer shell is slotted and bulged outward, which produces a springy effect, and if the shell is pushed into the barrel of the shotgun, it will fit closely and will not fall out or shift. The rifled steel barrel of the shell is provided with an extractor, so constructed that it will adjust itself to any ejector (common automatic) found on single- or double-barrel shotguns. Thus, by opening the gun, the empty cartridges will be ejected in the same manner as an ordinary shell. The rifled bullet shells are made so exact and accurate, and everything so thoroughly tested, that they will prove in every respect as reliable as a rifle, and with proper sighting can be used with single- and double-barrel shotguns at target practice.

**Targeting Shotguns**—10- and 12-gauge shotguns are targeted at 40 yards; 16-gauge guns at 35 yards.

**Sighting a Rifle Correctly at Targets**—Hold rifle firmly to shoulder, without strain or tremor; sights perfectly upright. The center of the notch in the rear sight should then be brought into direct alignment with the front sight; and when correctly held the tip of the front sight should appear about $\frac{1}{32}$ of an inch above the bottom of the notch of the rear sight, or so much as may be distinctly seen without blurring. With a bead or pinhead front sight the whole of the bead should be seen. Keeping the sights in the same relative position, the muzzle of the rifle should be raised until the tip of the front sight reaches the bottom edge of the bull's-eye, but does not quite touch it; a small space intervening just perceptible to the eye without straining. With aperture front sights, the aperture in the bead should "ring" the bull's-eye, allowing a thin white ring to show equally around the bull's-eye.

Variation in grouping shots is due to difference of holding the sights, firing with varied pulls of the trigger, etc.; and defective eyesight, farsightedness, nearsightedness, etc.; in which case the sights should be altered to the shooter's method of sighting. If this is done, it should be remembered as a general rule, that however the adjustment of the rear sight may be changed, the effect will cause the rifle to shoot in the direction toward which the rear sight has been moved, *while any alteration of the front sight produces an opposite effect*; as an example, if the rear sight moved toward the right, the rifle will shoot further to the right on the target; while if the *front sight is moved to the right, it will shoot to the left*; if the front sight is filed off or made lower, it will shoot higher, and so on.

**Trajectory or Flight of Rifle Bullets**—The path that a bullet follows, called its trajectory, from the instant of leaving the muzzle of a rifle until it strikes the target, is a continuous curve, no portion of which is a straight line. This curved path is due to the force of gravity acting in a downward direction upon the bullet, which deflects it more and more, as the range increases, from the straight line in which it was projected upon leaving the rifle. The bullet is deflected still further by the resistance of the air, which tends to increase the curvature of its trajectory by retarding its velocity. This effect is most noticeable when firing at long ranges. In order to determine the killing zone of any bullet, it is customary to give the midrange height of its trajectory, which is the height of the bullet above the straight line from muzzle of the rifle to the point where the bullet strikes the target.

**Fire Promptly**—Long-drawn or long-aimed shots make unsteady, inaccurate shooting; uncertainty is responsible for many misses and errors.

**Don't Experiment**—With ammunition, leave that for experts to do.

**Don't Leave**—Loaded firearms around camp or anywhere else.

**Don't Pass**—A loaded gun to a brother hunter or anyone.

**Don't Climb**—A fence with a loaded gun in your hand.

**Don't Let**—Your hammers rest on the plungers.

**Don't Go**—Hunting without a good reliable broken shell extractor, or without fitting your cartridges into the chamber, proving them.

**Don't Shoot**—With one eye closed; learn to keep them both open.

**Don't Let**—Your gun remain dirty overnight; but also never polish it so it shines.

**Don't Use**—Too much oil in the action of a gun or it will gum and stick.

**Don't Let Rust**—Stay in the barrels, it will eat a hole in them.

**Don't Vary**—From powder manufacturers' directions if reloading cartridges yourself.

**Don't Put**—A poor shell in your cartridge belt, better throw it away.

**Don't Use**—Shotgun powder for rifle cartridges or *high-pressure* powder in *low-pressure* cartridges.

**Don't Fail**—To smoke your sights if they are worn or shiny.

**Don't Approach**—Any wounded game without a cartridge in the chamber of your rifle, ready for any surprise.

**Don't Carry a Loaded Gun**—With hammers down; it's dangerous.

**Don't Try to Do**—Accurate shooting with a dirty gun—you can't.

**To Carry a Gun**—The safest way is on either shoulder, muzzle up. When hunting and when game is apt to be "flushed" any time, in the hollow of the left arm; never carry it muzzle toward a companion or dog; better under the arm so as the muzzle will point to the ground a few feet ahead of you, so as to rest your hands.

**Learning to Aim**—Tie a sheet of paper to a long string and secure it where a strong wind will swish it in motion and practice sighting at the moving paper; it's better than aiming at a still object. Don't snap the hammer uselessly.

**To Clean a Foul Gun or Leaded Barrel**—Pour in a little quicksilver, shaking it about; the quicksilver and lead will form an "amalgam" and clean the barrels thoroughly. Never clean leaded barrels with emery cloth.

**Use Fresh Beef Tallow**—As a rust preventative. If through with your gun for the season, insert in the barrels a "nick plug" or fill barrels with pure tallow or fresh beef fat.

**To Learn Distances**—Practice estimating distances as you go along from one object to another, counting your steps or paces; if your regular step, for instance, is 24 inches, 100 steps is 200 feet; practice this, estimating as you walk along, selecting objects say 200 to 300 yards distant; when the time comes for you to estimate distance quickly, such practice as this will enable you to come pretty close to being right. This is the military method of practice in estimating distances. Measure your regular pace and use same as a guide.

**Oil for Guns, Rifles, Etc.**—Sperm oil or fat of grouse is excellent.

**To Restore Color to Sights, Etc.**—Even small parts of a gun or rifle can be colored by holding in a gas flame until the color appears, then dipped in cold water.

**Stain or Coloring for Barrels, Etc.**—1 ounce muriate tincture of steel, 1 ounce spirits of wine, ¼ ounce muriate of mercury, ¼ ounce of nitric acid, ⅛ ounce blue stone, 1 quart water; allow to stand for several weeks or more to amalgamate. Clean well and remove grease, oil, etc. with lime and water. Lay on the liquid with a sponge every few hours, until a sort of rust appears, then rub it off with a wire scratch brush; continue the treatment until the color suits you, then wash well in boiling water and rub the barrels well until nearly cool (an excellent brown color).

**Use to Polish the Stocks**—Of rifles or guns, simply raw linseed oil (not boiled) rubbed well in, then polished.

**The Life of a Rifle Barrel**—The rifling in a barrel lasts for about 2,000 to 3,000 rounds.

**Saving Shells for Reloading**—Keep them clean and dry, wash well in hot soapsuds and water, rinse in very hot water, and be sure to drain and dry well; the heat of the hot water will dry them if drained well. Never reload a shell that has corroded parts.

**Don't Use**—Reloaded rifle ammunition for hunting; it's often unreliable. Select the very newest and best, unless you reload *yourself*.

**Never Start Out on a Hunting Trip**—Without chambering your cartridges that go to your belt, thus avoiding misfits. Use poor shells for killing wounded game.

**Use the Cartridges**—From the rear of your cartridge belt, keeping the nearest ones handy for an emergency.

**In a Tight Place**—Keep a cartridge or two in your left hand ready for quick action, and keep your magazine full.

**Smokeless Powders**—Are divided in two classes, low and high pressure. The first named being mostly used in old powder cartridges, the latter for cartridges of the military type.

**The 30–30 U.S A. Cartridge**—Has a breech pressure of 40,000 pounds to the square inch, the 236 Navy nearly 50,000 pounds.

**In Using Hollow-Point Bullets**—Fill the hole or hollow with wax, tallow, or soap.

**For Long-Distance Shooting**—Don't use express or hollow-point bullets.

**For Fine Target Shooting**—Use patched bullets.

**How to Find Out the Twist of Rifling**—Lubricate the inside of the barrel well. Take a bullet that is large enough to fit snugly so as to get a full impression of the rifling. Force it through the barrel carefully. Get a piece of straight wire smaller than the bore of the rifle; drill a hole in the bullet and fasten one end of the wire to it; shove the bullet with the wire fastened to it from the muzzle to the commencement of the rifling at the chamber.

Fasten the barrel in a vise or otherwise; make a chalk mark on the breech and muzzle of the barrel, also one on the wire in the alignment with those on the barrel. Make a mark on the wire even with the muzzle, and force the bullet toward the muzzle, and when the chalk mark on the wire has turned completely around, and is again in a line with those on the barrel, measure the number of inches the mark on the wire has traveled from the muzzle of the barrel, and you will find what you are looking for. The rifling of a barrel is from two- to five-thousandths of an inch deep.

**In Cold or Winter Weather**—Guns or rifles should be wiped dry of oil and not brought or put in a warm place; but left until through using out of doors or somewhere in a cold and safe convenient place.

**Never Reload**—Smokeless powder cartridges, never compress smokeless powder; it's dangerous.

**Never Jerk**—The trigger of a rifle or gun when firing; a steady pull with the gun held firmly to the shoulder is correct. Study and observe the faults and points of each shot.

**Killing Range of Revolvers**—A good revolver will kill at 50 to 100 yards.

**Crook of Stock**—Generally a tall person or one with long arms needs a gun with a long and crooked stock, and *vice versa*. A too straight stock makes a gun shoot high; a too crooked stock makes it shoot low.

**Length of Barrels**—The shorter the barrel the greater the range of divergence of the charge. Long barrels shoot closer than short, and will kill game at a greater distance. For quick shooting, and cover shooting, 28 to 30 inches is about right in a 12-bore. Short barrels should be charged with a finer grade of powder than longer ones.

**If Cornered by a Savage Beast**—And have the misfortune of having your gun or rifle rendered useless, making a hand-to-hand fight necessary, try and wrap a garment, coat (anything) around your left hand or arm or take a stick or club in that hand, leaving your right hand free for your knife, club, or revolver, and thrust the stick or club that is in the left hand into the mouth of the beast. All wild animals vent their spite on the objects nearest them; hence tamers of wild animals allow them to vent their spite on a staff or rod thrust into their face or teeth causing the animal to vent its spite on the object nearest them, and which they think is part of yourself *because it moves*; even a cat or dog will do this, as it's animal nature. So use the left hand to detract the animal's attention or rage, keeping the right free for the *attack*.

**At Short Range**—Always aim low, the tendency is to overshoot; aim at below and behind the shoulder, a vital spot.

**If Pursued by Game**—Or wild animals, aim to dodge instead of running from it. Don't turn your back to it, face and dodge the danger or you are a goner sure. All animals are more or less afraid of man and even a bear will run from a man unless forced to stand his ground. They will rarely provoke a fight and will run even from a barking dog; when wounded or forced to fight, only *a most fatal wound* is effective. The writer has personally seen on my Arctic voyages a polar bear shot with .45-caliber bullets in eleven different parts of his body and still keep on fighting desperately and I am informed by the best of authorities that it is by no means an infrequent affair. Tenacity of life is surprisingly evident in all large and savage animals, so act accordingly. Don't think because they fall that you are sure of them. The shock stuns them, but they soon recover, so never approach them except with extreme cautiousness, fully prepared for a sudden and most furious attack. Don't be overconfident.

**For Marsh Duck Shooting**—Use grass-color rubber or waterproof canvas hat and coat and rubber boots.

**Large Game Charge**—For 12-gauge guns 3½ drams power; 1 ounce No. 1 or 2 shot, or mixed.

**In Trailing Grouse**—Approach them as if ignorant of

their proximity, and shoot the instant you can; side shots are best; try and walk as though you did not see him, and he will not fly as quickly as though you come straight towards him.

**Wild Ducks Flying**—Travel over 100 feet in a second; if 50 yards away he will travel 15 feet in the time it takes for shot to reach him; hence the aim should be nearly 15 feet ahead; in windy weather they fly low.

**Always Set Decoys**—To windward of the blinds, and these had best be made *before the season;* ducks avoid any new or strange structures, are very wary of them.

**A Good Blind**—A rubber blanket to lay on and yourself hidden by grass, rushes, etc., until near enough to rise and shoot quick, or cover yourself with grass-color canvas.

**Use Waterproof Paper Shells**—For duck shooting; wet will not impair their fitting qualities.

**Corduroy Clothing**—Or canvas if drab color is all right for any kind of hunting, except "still hunting"; it's useless for that.

**To Secure Good Results**—Get ammunition made expressly for the gun you use or make your own. *(See Ideal Reloading Tools.)* Ammunition of other makes will do, but it is assuredly better to use ammunition made and intended for the very gun you use.

**Use Warm Wristlets**—Woolen ones for duck shooting in cold weather.

**A Few Loads of Buckshot**—May prove valuable in hunting with shotguns (handy for big game) but not for a full-choke gun unless loaded and shot well wadded by yourself. *(See To Shoot Buckshot elsewhere.)*

**Killing Range of a 12-Bore Gun**—Use a lead bullet that will pass easily and freely into the muzzle when covered with *a cloth patch*. Place a heavy wad under the ball, a light one over it; the patch should hold the ball to the center of the shell.

**In Using Buckshot**—It is well to use a few small shot in the spaces between the buckshot, or use bone dust.

**Woods Used in Gunpowder**—Manufactured in the form of charcoal are black alder, poplar, willow, and dogwood.

**For a Quick Shooter**—Modified choke is best; for a slow shot full choke.

**Wild Geese**—Are regular in going to and from their feeding grounds, so take advantage of the fact.

**For Teal Duck**—Use No. 7 or 8 shot, and aim well ahead always; if rising, hold above them; if drifting, hold under.

**To Moisten Dry Gun**—Breathe occasionally through the barrels of it or moisten the end of your cartridge.

**In Flock Shooting**—Select the leading or ahead bird; don't shoot at the center of the flock lest you hit only a straggler.

**Good Shotgun Target**—A barrel head hung by heavy wire and swung hard from the branch of a high tree (swing quickly).

**Prairie Chickens**—Frequent stubble fields in early morn or evening, near sloughs at midday.

**Hunter's and Fisherman's Lunch**—Get two flat stones, and then gather sufficient wood. Into the fire the stones go, and the wood is heaped about them. Soon the intense glow of live wood embers indicates that the time has come. A quail, snipe, or trout (a sliver of bacon in each) are placed on one of the stones, first well dusted of its ashes, and the other stone is laid upon them. Now the hot embers are raked about and over the stones, and the lunch is spread on the big rock near the spring. O, ye epicures, who think nothing good except served by a Delmonico or a Sherry, go ye into the mountains or trail, follow a brook for half a day, get wet, tired, and hungry, sit down and eat these cooked on the spot, and learn of the choice morsels of the hunter's, trapper's, and fisherman's art.

**Gun for Pigeon Shooting**—Select a 12-bore right barrel cylinder, and left full choke, chambered to stand heavy charges, or both barrels modified choke.

**Never Loan Your Gun or Rifle**—Lest you lose a friend.

**Distance Covered by Game**—In ⅛ of a second:

| | |
|---|---|
| 12 miles an hour | 2.2 feet. |
| 20 miles an hour | 3.6 feet. |
| 30 miles an hour | 5.5 feet. |
| 40 miles an hour | 7.3 feet. |
| 60 miles an hour | 11 feet. |

**Don't Fail to Sight Your Gun**—On an "out-of-range bird"; it's practice aiming even, if nothing else.

**Don't Approach Game**—From the windward side; get to the leeward of them.

**Don't Forget to Aim**—Under a bird that is alighting, or over them if arising, ahead of them if flying straight.

**Don't Aim and Fire Carelessly**—Or too quickly; rattled, excited, rapid shooting seldom counts; deliberation and carefulness are what bring accuracy and success.

**Don't Overshoot**—The tendency of most sportsmen is to do this; better low than too high.

**Don't Fail**—To cut the throats of dead game and draw the entrails if you wish to have good meat.

**Don't Blame the Gun**—They are seldom at fault; it's the man behind.

**Don't Forget**—That extreme care and quietness are essential when hunting, "stalking" especially.

**Don't Target Practice**—On a hunting trip, unless you are after encumbering yourself needlessly.

**Don't Sit**—On the bare ground; better to sit on your hat.

**Don't Forget**—To speak a good word for this book, for it deserves it.

**The Best Repeating Shotgun**—For field shooting, Winchester 12-gauge brush gun, 5 shot; 26-inch barrel; 7¼ pounds, model 1897, takedown, or model 1901, cylinder or modified choke bored.

**To Test a Shotgun**—So as to determine its accuracy or carrying abilities, chalk a target on a 30-inch circle 40 yards away, and note if the percentage of shot entering the circle is as follows: cylinder bore, 40 percent; modified choke, 50 percent; full choke, 60 percent; this is a good average. This is the gunmaker's pattern test, with ordinary or standard loads. By now increasing or decreasing your charges or loads, your distance, size of target, etc., you can determine to a nicety just how your gun shoots, enabling you to correct any existing faults before starting out on a trip.

**Use Decoys**—To leeward of your blinds, if in any way possible.

**In Wing Shooting**—Always keep your gun moving with the bird, sighting well ahead, from a few inches to a few feet, according to the distance and speed of the bird, and direction it is traveling.

### Slow Pull of Trigger *(6 Seconds)*

| Distance of Bird | Flight of Bird During Transit of Shot | Lateral Movement of Gun Muzzle by the Shooter |
|---|---|---|
| 15 yds. | 6 ft. 6 in. | 6.6 inches |
| 20 yds. | 7 ft. 7 in. | 5.7 in. |
| 25 yds. | 8 ft. 8 in. | 5.2 in. |
| 30 yds. | 9 ft. 9 in. | 4.9 in. |
| 35 yds. | 11 ft. | 4.8 in. |
| 40 yds. | 12 ft. 6 in. | 4.7 in. |
| 45 yds. | 13 ft. 10 in. | 4.7 in. |
| 50 yds. | 15 ft. 9 in. | 4.7 in. |

### Quick Pull of Trigger *(2 Seconds)*

| | | |
|---|---|---|
| 15 yds. | 3 ft. 8 in. | 3.7 in. |
| 20 yds. | 4 ft. 8 in. | 3.5 in. |
| 25 yds. | 5 ft. 8 in. | 3.4 in. |
| 30 yds. | 6 ft. 11 in. | 3.4 in. |
| 35 yds. | 8 ft. 2 in. | 3.5 in. |
| 40 yds. | 9 ft. 7 in. | 3.6 in. |
| 45 yds. | 11 ft. | 3.7 in. |
| 50 yds. | 12 ft. 9 in. | 3.8 in. |

*Note—One second of time allowed for a passage of shot through the barrels.*

## BEST TIME TO LOCATE DUCKS

October, November, moonlight nights; best time to shoot them is during heavy winds; best place to find them is in smooth or sheltered waters, or on the edges of sheltered woods. Best way to approach them at these times is against the wind, creeping up slowly, quietly and unobserved, lest they hear, see, or scent you. Better spend more time looking for their favorite spots and flights than in waiting for them to approach blinds or decoys (except in flight shooting.)

**When Using Decoys**—Always set them to the *leeward* of your blinds; arrange them so as their heads are anchored toward the wind. Do not group them close, but scatter them well.

**Do Not Recommend**—The 30–30 caliber rifle (except for small- game hunting). It should not be used for large game. Choose instead the 303 always in preference to the 30–30, *for the reason that the bullet of the 303* fits the barrel more accurately, will show greater penetration and velocity, and is even more accurate than the 30–30. These are facts borne out by experience, honestly given. The 30–30 is a good rifle, *but not for large game*.

**Best Rifle for Squirrels**—.22 caliber repeating rifle. Best place to find them is about beech or chestnut trees and high grounds. Best time, fall of year; hours, around sunrise and sunset; worst time, midday.

**Woodcock**—Best time, toward evening or very early morning (dawn). Best places: moist places near edge of lowlands, swamps, etc., north side of hills, etc. (the moist sides).

**Best Time for Quail**—Midday of sunshiny days, October and November. Best places, middle of fields, around small stubble or brush, or at edge of woods. Best way, with a good pointer dog.

**Best Time for Ducks**—October and November, early morn (daybreak) or early dusk. Best place about feeding grounds, around edges of marshes, or in sheltered woods, along its borders.

**Grouse or Partridge**—Best time, early morning, stormy or cold weather. Best places, around berry bushes, etc.; look for their regular roosts toward night.

**To Test Your Powder**—Lay a small pinch on a sheet of white paper and apply a match. If it flames instantly, leaving the paper clean and unscorched, it is good. Or rub a grain or two between the fingers; if they don't break or soil the fingers its quality is good.

**How to Become a Crack Shot**—The whole secret is in discovering the faults of each shot and correcting them before firing another shot.

**Always Practice**—Both snap- and deliberate shooting or aiming. Snap-shooting is raising the gun quickly, aiming, and firing as quick as the object is sighted, not waiting or wasting a second. Deliberate shooting is of course taking deliberate and careful aim.

**Excellent Practice**—Lay the rifle on the ground loaded, throw tiny paper bags of flour weighted with a stone high into the air; quickly get your gun and hit them before they reach the ground. If you have this done for you, keep your back to the thrower and only turn around and shoot at the signal to do so. This is excellent practice for the eye, hand, distance, flight, quickness, etc.

**Cheap Guns**—Make poor shots and poor sportsmen.

**Learning to Aim Well**—First, select an object to aim at. Second, throw up the gun with your eyes shut toward the object; when the gun touches your shoulder, open your eyes and see where your gun points; practice this getting your gun into line quickly. Third, fire at the object without a moment's hesitation, and note carefully the results, correcting any faults that exist.

**Mercurial Ointment**—Will cleanse leaded barrels.

**Always Practice Shooting**—With the same class of ammunition that you hunt with at the same loads exactly.

**Hold the Butt Firmly**—To the shoulder when firing, always when aiming and firing.

**Too Much Powder**—To ascertain if your charges contain too much powder, lay sheets of paper (white) 10 to 15 feet from the muzzle of the gun and fire it; if the paper catches grains of unconsumed powder, you are using too much. Firing along the snow will give the same proof.

**Buckshot in Cylinder Bores**—If it is desirable to shoot buckshot from a cylinder bore, such size should be selected as will chamber loosely in the bore—loading them in layers—three layers, with three shot in a layer. If it is desirable that they should scatter, place a card wad between each layer; if close shooting is desired, pour melted tallow over the shot after they are arranged in the shell.

**Buckshot and Ball in Choke Bores**—Bullets, buckshot and all shot larger than No. 1 should not be discharged from a choke bore. Ball may be shot from some choke bores a thousand times without injury; but there is *always* liability of jamming and no one can tell when it may occur. To use buckshot in a choke bore, when you are willing to risk consequences, place a wad in the muzzle and press it down to the point where the choke is closest. Then by chambering the shot on the wad there, determine the proper number to use in a layer in the shell.

**Wire Cartridges**—They may be used in a cylinder bore for long-range shots, but do not give good results when used in a choke bore.

**Tight Wads**—A tight wad over the shot makes the shot scatter.

**To Make a Gun Scatter**—To make a shotgun scatter, divide the shot charge into three or four portions and place a card wad between each portion.

**Killing Range of a Gun**—Forty to fifty yards is the killing range of a 12-gauge shotgun with ordinary loads.

**In Shooting Flying or Running Game**—Aim well in advance of the object so as to allow for the distance traveled by the game during the interval between pulling the trigger and the shot reaching its destination. A few inches or feet according to speed of movement. *(See Speed of Birds' Flights.)*

## MISCELLANEOUS TRAPPERS' AIDS

**The Best Bear Bait**—Is honey smeared on fresh fish, or burnt honeycomb.

**A Splendid Place for a Trap**—Is between two logs where there is a passageway through which the animal must pass: by-paths, as they are termed, natural channels, crevices or paths littered with hollow logs, etc., through which the animal must pass, or is apt to.

**Never Handle Traps**—With bare hands; use rags or buckskin gloves. Never spit about where traps are laid.

**Use Scent Baits**—Wherever possible. Barkstone, fish oil, castorium, musk, asafetida, oil of rhodium, oil of skunk, amber, anise, sweet fennel, cummin, fenugreek, lavender, or a compound of them all.

**Soak a Piece of Meat**—In the scent compound and drag it along on the ground between your run of traps; it is very effective as a trail to the trap, leading animals to them.

**Clogs Used on Traps**—Should never be secured to a tree or stake; let it be a stone or log of size and weight equal to the game you desire to trap; fasten it so it cannot be jerked off.

**Always Place Your Traps**—Where you can inspect them with the least difficulty. Animals often visit traps a dozen times, smelling them suspiciously and leaving them by reason of that suspicion. If your traps are right, never touch or change them. If a storm or blizzard comes, snow and cold in plenty, you will then get your reward, as the snow covers the suspicious part and the cold makes them hungry enough not to be too particular.

**Trapper Packs**—Including traps, have the limit of weight at about 65 to 75 pounds.

**For Trapping Deer**—Use the New House No. 4; for Skunk, No. 2.

**In Baiting Traps**—Always place the bait either on stick above the trap or in an enclosure, so arranged as the animal must step on or run over the trap, or better yet, jump up to get it; never place it on the pan.

**Quantity of Traps to Take**—Depends on the locality you trap in. If you travel by boat or team your supply need not be limited, but if you intend to make a business of trapping, the more the better.

**Season of Trapping**—November to April. Furs from May to September are useless. Winter furs only are in prime.

**Always Set Traps**—For aquatic animals where they can take to the water, and by weight of the traps and chains drown themselves.

**To Make Fish Oil**—The scent used by many old trappers. Take trout, eels, or fat fish of any kind, cut in small pieces and put them in bottles, and leave in hot sun, when an oil and putrid smell accumulates. Use this to scent your bait.

**Bird or Fish Heads Are Good Bait**—In cold weather. Smoke your baits to give them a stronger smell, or smear your traps with blood, using a feather to smear it over them. Fried meats smeared with honey are good trap bait.

**Use**—No. 5 or 6 Newhouse traps for bear, moose, etc. No. 4½ for wolf. No. 2½ for otter.

**An Indian Method in Winter**—Of killing wild game, wolves, bears, etc. is to take a piece of flexible steel or whalebone, anything that has a bend to it, and bend it into as small a circle as possible, securing it with the sinews of a deer; this they insert in a ball of meat, flesh, fat, and blood and allow the whole ball (not a large one) to freeze. A number of these they will throw out on the snow or ice, about the haunts of the animals; coming along they find them, on account of their being hard and frozen. The heat of the stomach soon melts the frozen parts of flesh and sinews, when the spring coil straightens out, piercing the stomach, causing agony and death, which in due time ensues, and by following the trail of the animal they invariably find them, perhaps locating others besides.

**To Make Traps Rustproof**—Dip them in a solution of melted beeswax and rosin.

**Set Traps Whenever Possible**—In the runways of paths of animals.

**In Rutting Season**—Use for skunk bait musk of skunk or rotten eggs with old meat.

**A Practical Trap**—Can be made by boring a series of two-inch or larger auger holes in a waterlogged stump or log and driving in two or three horseshoe nails, so that any small-headed animal who thrusts in his head to secure bait behind the nails cannot withdraw his head, because the nails catch and kill him.

**Set Traps for Otter**—At the foot of their slides a trifle under the water. Beaver also.

**The Secret of Trapping Wild Animals**—My style of setting traps was most simple and very effective, although it required a good many traps to do the work. Knowing the habits of the animals I was trying to catch alive, I adopted the following methods.

I set my traps only on the trails running through the thickest part of the woods. Here we would bury traps at intervals along the path by first digging a hole with a hatchet and removing the earth. Then we carefully laid a trap in place, laying a piece of canvas under the trap pan to keep the earth from interfering with the spring or clogging it. Next we carefully covered the trap with earth and smoothed the ground off, after securing the trap chain to the limb of a bush or trunk of a tree. We were careful to place a few branches on either side of the path ahead of each trap to guide the animal directly over the trap into it.

Then all was ready but one thing and that was the secret of our great success in trapping animals. We placed a small stick across the path right in front of the trap. This served to guide the animal's foot directly onto the pan of the trap, as an animal in walking on a trail will never tread on a stick, but always take a short step without touching it. A stick placed at the right distance in front of the trap will always have the desired effect. All animals while prowling through the woods will follow a trail when they encounter one for some distance before taking to the woods again. Consequently a line of traps set at intervals of a few rods along the paths through the woods is pretty sure to land any wandering animal.

—"Buzzacott"

**Wolves Will Not**—Touch dead game if it is partly covered with brush, leaves, etc., as they fear a trap.

**Always Suspend Your Bait**—A trifle over the trap so as the animal must step on the pan to secure it.

**Don't Ship Skins**—Unless caught in season and prime, and have them tanned right; for those, however, who are in the woods, away from shipping points, these receipts are mostly intended for.

**In Skinning Hides**—Keep the back of the knife close to the hide (always) and draw out the skin with the left hand, using a skinning knife to ensure success.

**To Salt Hides**—Remove flesh or excess fat, put on plenty of salt thick; when the salt is absorbed put on more, roll up tight fur side out, cord it, and it is ready to ship.

**To Catch Muskrat**—In the female muskrat, near the genitals, is a small bag that holds 30 to 40 drops. All the trapper has to do is to procure a few female muskrats and squeeze the contents of the bag into a vial. Now, when in quest of muskrats, sprinkle a few drops of the liquid on the bushes over and around the trap. This will attract the male muskrats in large numbers, and if the traps are properly arranged, large numbers of them may be taken.

**Large Game or Whole Deer**—Should never be skinned for shipment; draw the entrails, wash inside with cold water.

> Grotesquely detailed advice on how to gut and dress a deer may be found in *A Man's Life: The Complete Instructions.*

**Game Birds**—Should be shipped in natural state, undrawn, in cold weather; in hot weather draw as soon as killed if to be shipped.

**Never Dry Skins by a Fire**—It ruins and spoils them.

**Weight of Traps Per Dozen**—(Newhouse) No. 0, 7 lbs.; No. 1, 10 lbs.; No. 1½, 13 lbs.; No. 2, 17 lbs.; No. 3, 28 lbs.; No. 4, 33 lbs.; No. 4½, 98 lbs.

**Right Traps to Use**—No. 0, rat or gopher; No. 1, muskrat; No. 1½, mink; No. 2, fox; No. 2½ and 3, otter; No. 4, beaver; No. 4½, wolf; No. 5, bear; No. 6 (for grizzly bear, lions, tigers, cougars) it is the strongest trap made, weight 45 lbs.

**A Unique Trap**—Cut a small bush (spruce or pine is best), stick it up in deep snow or through the ice of a small river or stream; such a curious thing will attract animals to it, being new to them. Small pieces of meat, and several traps placed here and there about it, are pretty sure to land an animal or two after a few nights. Set your main bait, which should hang so as the animal must put his foot on the pan of the trap to reach it.

**Another One**—Bore holes in the ground and fill them with bait scented, in a circle, your trap in the center; this is mighty apt to catch something, especially if two natural logs V shape lay near it. It is sure death to wolves if the bait is poisoned and frozen.

**Burning Sulfur or Brimstone**—Placed in the hole of any animal will smother them out or kill them.

**All Water Animals**—Are prime while ice is in the rivers or streams.

**Clean and Smoke Your Traps**—Using smoke from feathers of birds. Never handle them with bare hands. Wash them well and oil them first.

**Wash Traps**—With weak lye or soapsuds, then grease

and smoke them over burnt feathers, and never touch them with your hands.

**Unseasonable Furs**—Are graded 2, 3, or 4, last grades, and are only prime No. 1 in early winter.

**When Traps Are Set**—Smear with a feather your *scent* baits over it, and you are almost sure of *success*.

**Use Buckskin or Moosehide Moccasins**—When hunting or trapping; and do not stir up the ground when setting traps; be careful to leave the ground as near as you found it as possible to do.

**Tanning Fur and Other Skins**—*First*: Remove the legs and other useless parts and soak the skin soft; then remove the flesh substances and soak in warm water for an hour, now:

Take for one large or two or three small skins, borax, salt-peter and Glauber's salt, of each ½ ounce and dissolve or wet with soft water sufficiently to allow it to be spread on the flesh side of the skin.

Put it on with a brush, thickest in the center or thickest part of the skin, and double the skin together, flesh side in, keeping it in a cool place for twenty-four hours, not allowing it to freeze, however.

*Second*: Wash the skin clean, and then: Take sal-soda, 1 ounce; borax, ½ ounce; refined soap, 2 ounces (white hard soap); melt them slowly together, being careful not to allow them to boil, and apply the mixture to the flesh side as at first—roll up again and keep in a warm place for 24 hours.

*Third*: Wash the skins clean, as above, and have saleratus 2 ounces, dissolved in hot rainwater sufficient to well saturate the skin, then:

Take alum, 4 ounces; salt, 8 ounces; and dissolve also in hot rainwater; when sufficiently cool to allow for handling of it without scalding, put in the skin for 12 hours; then wring out the water and hang soaking. Let dry. Repeat from 2 to 4 times according to the desired softness of the skin when finished.

*Lastly*: Finish by pulling, working, etc., and finally by rubbing with piece of pumice stone and fine sandpaper.

This works admirably on sheepskins as well as on fur skins, dog, cat, or wolf skins also, making a durable leather well adapted to washing.

**A Novel and Effective Poison Trap**—For skunk, etc. Bore holes in logs, then fill with lard, tallow, etc., to which strychnine has been mixed. When it freezes they must lick it out, and it kills them before they can get far away. Scent the spot so as to attract them to it.

**Always Bed Your Traps**—On bare, smooth ground, then cover with dry leaves or dirt or both; never use twigs on the pan; that is for the foot of the animal only.

**Fasten Small Traps**—To cut a branch of a tree about the weight of the animal you expect, using the same branch if need be, to adjust your bait over the trap, but rather choosing a natural bush or tree. Never set a trap until the last thing.

**For Signs of Animals**—Dung, signs of a meal, feathers, bones, etc., shed hair, holes, dens. Set traps here.

**Preserve Leavings**—When you find feathers, etc., leavings of a meal, keep them to use in connection with coverings of the trap you set, or set a trap about it.

**Skunk in Fall**—Are often found in open fields, about small bushes, etc. In winter on higher ground.

**A Good Dog**—Is a trapper's valuable adjunct; always aiding you to locate trails, dens, etc.

**Good Baits**—Are birds, fish, beef, offals, rabbits, cheese, rotten eggs, entrails, etc.

**Trapper's Patience**—Study it; don't pull up a trap, try again and again; stick right to good places.

**Opossums, Coons, Etc.**—Are found in dense woods.

**In Setting Traps in Holes**—Insert them well inside and scent them; don't place them outside, they can perceive the fraud. Cover with leaves.

**Bait Gone**—When you find this, and trap still set, arrange your bait on the other side of trap; leave the trap be.

**Mink Can be Found**—Near swamps, along streams and their waterways, especially where dead wood, logs, etc. are bunched. Look for their tracks in the mud, sand, etc.

**To Find Out**—Positively if animals frequent a certain spot, place a small piece of bait there overnight; if it is gone in the morning, set your trap right there carefully.

**In Dead of Winter**—Many animals hole up for several weeks or more.

**Never Apply Heat**—In drying skins; hang them in the shade is best.

**Useless Tails**—Tails of opossum and muskrat are of no value, so cut them off.

**Remove the Fat**—Of all skins; fat left on heats and spoils the hide.

**Best Month**—For bears and badgers is March; water animals until the ice breaks.

**To Trap Mink**—Dig a hole in the bank near their haunts, place your bait inside your trap at its edge, and cover it well; sprinkle water around so as to wash your traces away; before leaving it clog the trap of course, and use scent bait.

**To Catch a Wild Pig**—Note that a pig is as smart as a dog, so your hunting dogs may easily be outfoxed by a boar in flight. Men quick with a rope may lasso a pig. A covered pit with food left as bait in the middle of the cover will entrap the pig in the pit; however extreme caution must be employed in extracting the pig.

**Never Set**—Large traps without a trap wrench.

**The Best Time**—First stormy night, or before a storm; the animals are then foraging for food and seeking warm holes to den.

**How Animals Gnaw Loose**—The caught leg of foot becomes numb and somewhat painless, and the bone being broken, is easily detached.

**Mark Your Traps**—By filing your initial thereon, or by marks.

**When You Succeed**—In catching an animal, leave your trap and reset it; it often pays well, especially in dens.

**Always Remove**—Bones from tails of skinned animals; it rots therein otherwise.

**Keep Skins**—Loose and straight; don't roll them up; pack them straight is best.

**Skunks Are Easy**—To trap. A rabbit often displays more intelligence as to traps than the skunk.

**Bait for Mink**—Any fresh meats, fish or fowl, muskrat meat, etc.

**To Attract Wolves**—Place bones or large chunk of meat in fire and let it smolder. Use carcasses of other animals.

**Number of Traps to Use**—Six dozen traps are ample for any trapper to attend.

**Always Sink Your Traps**—To the exact level of the ground, leaving the surface as near as it was as possible.

**Cut Up Old Baits**—In small pieces and scatter them along the route of your traps.

**How to Skin**—Cat, fisher, fox, lynx, martin, mink, opossum, wolverine, otter, skunk, and muskrat must be "cased," that is, not cut open. In skinning, cut at the rump and turn the skin inside out over the body of the animal, leaving the pelt side out.

After scraping, cleaning, and drying, some dealers advise turning the skin back again, leaving the fur side out; but with the exception of foxes, red, silver, and cross, the large dealers now prefer the skin left pelt side out, as the quality can be more easily determined by examining the rumps; and are better preserved and protected in the numerous handlings.

Badger, bear, beaver, raccoon, and wolf must be "open," that is, cut up the belly from rump to head. After scraping, cleaning, and drying, stretch to a uniformly oblong shape to the fullest extent of the skin, but not so much as to make the fur thin. When thoroughly dry, trim off any little pieces that spoil the appearance of the skin, but leave on heads, noses, and claws.

> Instructions on how to skin a rabbit without using a knife may be found in *The Modern Man's Guide to Life,* available from our office.

**Do Skinning, Stretching, Etc.**—After you have tended all your traps. Skin and dry carefully if you market.

**Jerked Meats**—If you have the fortune to kill a deer or moose in warm weather, and have an oversupply of meat that is likely to be tainted, you can preserve it by the following process:

Cut all the flesh from the bones in thin strips, and place them for convenience on the inside of the hide.

Add three or four quarts of salt for a moose, and a pint and a half for a deer, well worked in.

Cover the whole with the sides and corners of the hide to keep out flies, and let it remain in this condition about two hours.

Drive four forked stakes into the ground so as to form a square of about eight or ten feet, leaving the forks four feet high. Lay two poles across one way in these forks, and fill the whole space the other way with poles laid on the first two, about two inches apart. The strips of flesh should then be laid across the poles, and a small fire of clean hardwood should be started underneath, and kept up for twenty-four hours. This process will reduce the weight of the flesh more than half, bringing it to a condition like that of dried or smoked beef, in which it will keep any length of time.

This is called jerked venison. It is good eating, and always commands a high price in market. An oversupply of fish can be treated in the same manner. They should be split open on the back, and the backbone taken out.

**Never Set**—Large traps without a trap clamp. Never place your hands about the jaws or pan, and don't handle a set trap.

**Trapper's Best Friend**—Is a good, well-trained dog.

**Don't Reset**—Where sprung traps are found; try a new place thereabout. If bait is gone and trap unsprung, you are at fault, so reset in these instances.

**Overhanging Trees**—Or inclined ones, nail your bait to them. If your traps are set under right, are excellent places.

**For Water-Set Traps**—(Traps set in water.) Use rubber boots and wade into the waters, avoiding the shores, or wash your tracks by throwing water on them.

**Dry-Set Traps**—(Traps set on land.) Step always in your same tracks, using moccasins, not boots, or cover boots with skin tied on hair side out.

**Use Dirt from Dens**—Rotten wood, leaves, dung, small feathers, etc. for bedding down traps.

**Wash Traps**—Oil and grease them well, smoke or cover with blood, beeswax, etc. and keep free from dust.

**Always**—Set your traps for the foot of the animal and arrange your bait so as he must set his foot on the pan to secure bait.

**No Duty**—On raw furs from Canada.

**Skunk**—Are the first animals to get prime in late fall and early winter. Water animals are last.

**Bears and Badgers**—Are only prime in midwinter and very early spring.

## HOW TO MAKE A CLAM BAKE

Get a pile of stones, a hundred or more, about one-half cobble size, flat as possible (any stones will do if flat ones are scarce); the rougher the plant the more the fun. Gather a bountiful supply of good hard-wood firewood, start a rousing bonfire. From this secure a deep, live bed of embers and coals (red hot), throwing your stones into the fire when the embers begin to form and let them get piping hot. When this is done right you are ready for the bake. Next take a pile of wet seaweed, sea grass, rushes, even wet green grass will do (but seaweed or sea grass is best) and over a layer of hot stones spread a layer of the seaweed, two or three inches deep, so as to make a steaming bed, then strew over it clams, sweet potatoes, green corn, etc. (if you wish, or clams only). If corn is used leave on a single husk, cover it all with seaweed and more stones, and let the mass steam and cook for forty-five minutes to one hour, or until the larger articles are well done. Watch it so it won't burn; if too hot or dry, souse it with water. With *green bark* plates, twigs, forked branches, etc. (never use plates, knives, etc. or you lose half the fun) go at it and help yourself, the more the merrier. Pepper, salt, vinegar, lemons, constitute the finishing ingredients for a feast worthy of the gods—try it.

## ASSORTED ADVICE FOR SPORTSMEN

**Weevils in Flour or Hard Bread**—Can be killed by placing same in a very hot oven for a few minutes.

**For Snow Blindness**—Charcoal rubbed about the cheeks and eyes relieves and prevents, or use smoked or blue or green glasses.

**To Remove Candle Grease**—From clothing in camp, take a hot spoon or iron of any kind, lay a piece of absorbent wrapping or blotting paper on the grease, press the hot iron over it, and it will clean the candle grease, removing it as slick as a whistle.

**Never Use Bullets**—Over 405 grains for large game hunting.

**A Flat Trajectory**—Is valuable in a hunting rifle, as it lessens the errors caused by the variations in distances incorrectly judged, and also obviates the necessity of frequent changes at various ranges, especially in the case of running game. Consequently, in selecting an arm for purely hunting purposes, it is desirable to obtain one with a reasonably low flight of bullets. Such a rifle will give good hunting results, although the same amount of accuracy cannot be obtained at the longer ranges or in shooting at known distances as with the rifle with higher trajectory. This is particularly true of the old-style ammunition, where the bullet has a tendency to fall off badly at longer ranges.

**Why Lost Hunters Travel in a Circle**—There have been many attempted explanations why lost people in the woods travel in a circle. The solution is, the lost one has his mind fixed that he must travel to the left or right (as the case may be); that fact being uppermost in his mind he continually inclines that way, resulting in his traveling in a circle. This can be avoided by selecting some distant object to guide himself by, and not losing sight of the same object. If at night select a bright star, as the sailor does. *(See article on Lost in Camp, and the advice on how to find your way out of the woods in* A Man's Life: The Complete Instructions.)

**To Make "Pemmican"**—That will keep. Take jerked or dried beef strips and pound them to a powder or pulp, mix with fat (warm), beef tallow, sugar, and raisins. Put in bladders or skins and tie up airtight. Used extensively by Arctic and other explorers, and if kept airtight will last for years.

**Penetration Is Necessary**—In order to give killing power to the bullet, enabling it to penetrate until it reaches a vital spot or strikes resistance when it can do damage. Generally speaking, a light charge of powder, with a comparatively heavy bullet, gives greater accuracy, while a heavy charge of powder with a comparatively light bullet gives higher velocity and flatter trajectory. A heavy bullet will give great penetration, while a bullet of lighter weight with a heavy powder charge is more apt to spread. In seeking after flat trajectory and high velocity with the old black-powder cartridges, some combinations were devised that secured these two objects, but accuracy was sadly wanting, as some of these cartridges could not make a group of ten successive shots at 200 yards in a circle of much less than 20 inches diameter. This was carrying the search to extremes. A rifle can hardly be considered very valuable for hunting purposes, except for some special styles of hunting, unless it can group its shots under reasonably favorable conditions in at least a 12-inch circle at 200 yards. For a hunting rifle, what we need is the *power,* so as to give the velocity, and consequently energy. Then we must seek a bullet to utilize this energy. There are two types of these bullets. One used to some extent by foreign sportsmen has a few metal cases, with the jacket split on the side so that it collapses on impact. The one most in vogue now is a metal-patched bullet, with soft lead point, which mushrooms on impact, and in this way has exactly the same effect on animal tissue as the large-caliber bullets, together with the advantage of a higher velocity.

**Still-Hunting for Deer**—The best time for still-hunting is in running time, in the months of October and November, after the does are with fawn and are running and hiding from the bucks. When you see a doe running through the woods, go and take your position in shooting distance of where she passed, and keep a sharp lookout the way she came, and often, in a very few minutes, you will see a buck coming, tracking her. Let him come up near enough for you to get a fair shot; bleat or whistle at him and he will stop. If you are a marksman, then you will have your venison. Still-hunting in the months of October and November is the most successful way of hunting. Sportsmen that are good rifle shots are the most successful still-hunting. Shotguns will do for driving, but rifles are the best to use in still-hunting.

**Positions at Different Ranges**—At 200 yards, stand up; at 300 yards, kneel or sit down; at all other ranges, sit or lay down, supporting the rifle by your elbows, or a bank, twig, etc.

**Deer and Moonlight**—Where deer are comparatively undisturbed, they feed nearly as much in the day as in the night, when the moon is up. If the moon has shown all night they will lie quiet all night. During the last quarter of the moon, when the moon has been down nearly all day, they become very hungry and feed nearly all night, so that is the best time to fire-hunt. If you wish to still-hunt, go when the moon rises or is yet up, whether forenoon or afternoon. If you hunt with dogs go at other times, as they will be sluggish and won't run far ahead of the hounds. The best time to fire-hunt is a dark, cloudy night when the moon is up.

**Use a Water Canteen**—As a hot water bottle on cold nights. It equals an extra blanket and will keep you warm all night.

**Pull of Triggers**—Test them for 4 to 4½ pounds for running game; on rifles about 2 pounds.

**A Barrel Head**—Makes an excellent moving target for a rifle when bowled like a hoop some distance away.

**Chalk Your Sight**—When hunting at night; smoke it if bright during a sunny day.

**Don't put oil on action parts of a gun or rifle in cold or freezing weather.** If you do the action will stiffen or freeze. Better wipe them dry and clean using no oil whatsoever.

**Frosty guns** or rifles after use on a freezing day are better left in a cold but safe place. Do not place them near a stove.

**Use a Wick Plug**—For your rifles or shotguns. It saves cleaning, prevents rust and pitting.

**High Winds and Dry Leaves**—Make poor hunting. Light, steady winds after rain is ideal hunting weather.

**To Find Water**—If on a plain, select a point that seems below the general level and dig especially where the most growth of vegetation appears. If in a rough country it is easier, as large hills store up water that can usually be dug for at their lowest base.

**A Horse**—Will drink sparingly of impure water or refuse it. A dog will drink any water no matter how impure. If water smells or tastes bad, go without it, unless well boiled first. Prickly pears or bruised cactus leaves will clarify water. It is unwise to drink when overheated. A pebble in the mouth relieves thirst.

**Hot Coffee**—Is a stimulant far more beneficial before hard work than the same quantity of whiskey.

**To Dry the Inside of Wet Boots or Shoes**—Soldiers or cowboys heat a pint or so of corn or oats and put them in overnight. Small pebbles do as well.

**Good Flypaper for a Tent**—Smear common paper with molasses. If too thin add a little sugar and heat it until thick enough.

**A Handkerchief**—Left in or tied to the carcass of fresh

killed game will keep flesh-eating animals away as they scent man.

**Deer and Salt Licks**—When you find a salt lick, use at night a reflector light to attract the game. For trapping deer use No. 4 Newhouse trap.

**Don't Use Imported Guns**—Be American. (No better guns made.) Put the difference in cost in ammunition and learn to be a good shot.

**Outfit for a Tramp Trip**—A pack sack with straps; 1 adjustable-handle frying pan; 1 heavy army quart cup, placed in stout coffeepot; 1 folding axe; 1 hunting knife; 1 compass; 1 waterproof matchbox (filled); chunk of bacon; bag of ground coffee mixed with sugar; small sack cornmeal and flour mixed; a few ounces of tea, salt, pepper; little baking powder (in waterproof bag); blanket and poncho (rubber) blanket; rifle and ammunition and a fairly full stomach before you start; and a lunch in your pocket. Weight about 30 pounds, pack about 24 inches by 18, and you can tramp from New England to Missouri. *Don't forget this book.*

**Choose Shoes That Fit**—Easily, as dew, moist grass, etc., shrinks and hardens them. Keep them well greased with tallow or fresh meat fat; it softens and helps them water off.

**Cure for "Mountain Fever"**—Wild sage brush made into a strong hot tea.

**If You Like This Book**—Send for others of a like spirit— *A Man's Life: The Complete Instructions; The Modern Man's Guide to Life; The Modern Woman's Guide to Life; The Modern Man's Guide to Modern Women;* and *Cowboy Wisdom.* If you find you are a woman, you may wish to consult *The Modern Woman's Guide to Life.* The five volumes, all bound neatly in paper, may be obtained from Modern Man Books, in care of Rex's Barber Shop, 116 W. Jefferson St.,

Mankato, Kansas, 66956. A discount of 10 percent is offered to those wishing to obtain three or more volumes. An excellent T-shirt made of pure American cotton is also offered. For particulars, contact the office at (913) 378-3772 during normal working hours.

**Purify Alkali Water**—By using a small lump of crystallized acetic acid.

**Best Hunting Hounds**—Are three-quarter foxhound and one-quarter staghound.

**How to Cross a Dangerous Stream**—There are four ways to cross a dangerous river or stream:

Pack or weight fording
Pole fording
Rope or raft fording
Animals must swim—the packed outfit won't spoil by a wetting. The chief point is to get the grub rations across and keep them dry. (This must be done.)

*Pack Fording*—Suppose the stream is 30 yards wide and you find a place where it is swift but not over waist deep; here your grub will help, for an 80-pound pack will hold you to the bottom, when without it you would be swept away. This fact is well known, and rocks or gravel from the bank will be useful if your pack is too light to hold you down. In this fording your pack must be well up on your shoulders and ready to drop quickly, for if you fall down with a tightly tied or strapped pack, you will not come up until you have lost interest in the undertaking. Frequently one can find an easy ford, but on occasions there will be no good crossing for several miles.

*Pole Fording*—If there are three or four in the party decide on the best ford, usually the widest stretch. Cut a slender pole between eight and twelve feet long, and at least three inches in diameter at the small end. You can find balsams or alders on almost any glacier stream except in high altitudes, where fording is usually easy, and the streams are small. It is good to undress as then there will be less resistance to the water, and you keep your clothes dry, but keep on your footgear, or the round glacial stones will grind your ankles. When all is ready, stand in line and grasp the pole.

The lightest man (A) should be on the upstream and heaviest man (B) on the downstream end of the pole. A's pack and clothes should be distributed between the others, as they need weight and A will be under water occasionally. Now all start across the line, working downstream, always keeping the pole parallel with the current.

As the water deepens, A may be swept from his feet, but he must hold on to the pole for he is making an eddy for the others to walk in. If possible, always pass below rocks; the water is deeper there but less swift than on the upstream side.

But in all fords remember that it is the fool who never turns back. If the water feels too strong, return while you can, for a glacier stream has no mercy.

*Raft Fording*—If in a timbered section with the outfit of tools, previously mentioned, raft building is an easy solution of the problem.

# Appendix I:
# Miscellaneous Outdoor
# Amusements

ⒼⅢⅢⓈ

If no other objects present themselves, and the weather is fair, make the object of your walk the location of a suitable pasture for the following outdoor enterprise:

## HOW TO PLAY REAL GOLF
## ON A FIVE-ACRE MEADOW

It is interesting for all lovers of golf to know that golf is being played on small links with a new ball in place of the hard ivory ball, which is used on large links. This ball was born of necessity, on the New England coast, and has filled a long-felt want.

Certain naval officers fond of golf found it difficult to get to the golf links to which they were invited at places visited by the fleet, and so were often deprived of much needed relaxation and exercise; whereupon Captain Wright, of the North Atlantic Squadron, devised a ball of cork (or pine) and improvised a course in a five-acre meadow where successful golf was played at ports visited by this squadron.

The ball might be utilized extensively by the vast army of people deprived of regular links by distance, expense, or want of time. The new ball of cork or of light wood is the

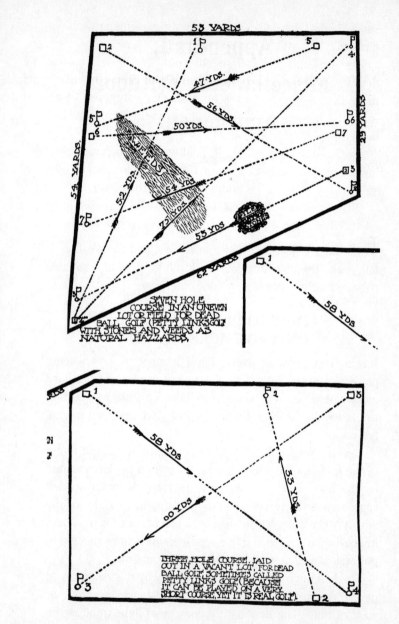

same size as the regulation ball, and when painted resembles it closely.

The principle involved is, of course, lightness, which deprives it of carrying power. As this ball cannot be driven more than 50 yards, it calls for a shorter course, and thus makes it possible to play the regular game on abbreviated links.

Any lawn or large lot or old field will do to begin on. The holes may be placed at 50, 74, or 100 yards apart, and be situated according to the ingenuity or taste of the player.

Where the ground will permit it, wooden clubs should be used, especially if the balls are of soft wood, as the irons split and scar them readily. Yet these balls are so cheap that their destruction is really of small moment.

These balls are not on the market, but persons who find it difficult to get them made of cork will find pine ones are easily made and might be turned in any carpenter shop where these is a lathe. Soft white pine will be found to be the lightest and most satisfactory material for a cheap and useful ball. They can be made at a ridiculously low price—say 15 cents per dozen.

The balls should be about 1¾ inches in diameter, or a shade less, and crisscrossed on the surface with the edge of a chisel.

To paint them stick a pin in lightly and submerge in a can of thin enamel paint (white) and suspend by a string attached to the pin until thoroughly dry.

Suggestions for layout of the links will be seen in the accompanying diagrams.

The advantages of this ball are the following:

No caddy is necessary (though always desirable), as the short distance enables the player to locate his lies easily, and the use of but one club (wooden driver) leaves no bag to carry.

For those seeking economy, it can be played at slight expense.

Convenience is its chief recommendation.

It affords both increased practice and exercise.

This ball "lofts" beautifully, and at the start sails away as promisingly as the heavier ball, so that the eye loses none of the delight experienced in a successful drive.

If it has a disadvantage it will be found in "putting" practice, where its lightness may prove disappointing at first.

But, taken all together, this ball is a real discovery, and will meet with favor and prove a boon generally.

And, to get to the meadow:

## Constructing a Bridge Across a Small Stream

For crossing a small creek or deep ditch a cheap bridge can be built as shown in the illustration.

The lumber used is 6 inches wide and 2 inches

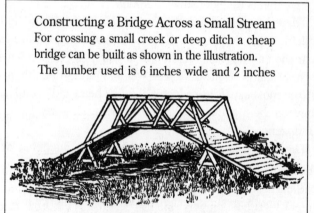

A BRIDGE OF TRIANGLES

thick, except for the floor and four side braces. Saw 11 pieces the length required for each of the two sides, then bore bolt holes 1½ inches from each end. Use ⅝-inch bolts 8½ inches long where four pieces come together and 6½-inch bolts where three pieces meet. The A-shaped supports and the pieces for the approaches are bolted on at

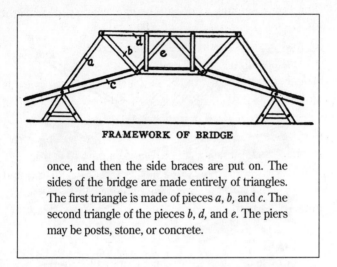

**FRAMEWORK OF BRIDGE**

once, and then the side braces are put on. The sides of the bridge are made entirely of triangles. The first triangle is made of pieces *a, b,* and *c.* The second triangle of the pieces *b, d,* and *e.* The piers may be posts, stone, or concrete.

## HOW TO MAKE A PAPER CANOE THAT CAN BE EASILY CARRIED

Now you might think it absurd to advise making a paper boat, but it is not, and you will find it in some respects and for some purposes better than the wooden boat. When it is completed you will have a canoe, probably equal to the Indian's bark canoe. Not only will it serve as an ideal fishing boat, but when you want to combine hunting and fishing you can put your boat on your shoulders and carry it from place to place wherever you want to go and at the same time carry your gun in your hand. The material used in its construction is inexpensive and can be purchased for a few dollars.

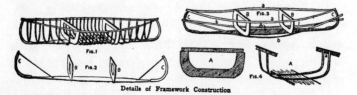

Details of Framework Construction

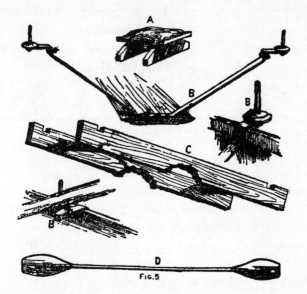

FIG.5

Make a frame (Fig. 1) on which to stretch the paper. A board 1 inch thick and about 1 foot wide and 11½ feet long is used for a keel, or backbone, and is cut tapering for about a third of its length, toward each end, and beveled on the outer edges (A, Fig. 2). The crossboards (B, Fig. 2) are next sawed from a pine board 1 inch thick. Shape these as shown by A, Fig. 4, 13 inches wide by 26 inches long, and cut away in the center to avoid useless weight. Fasten them crosswise to the bottom board as shown in Fig. 1 and 2, with long stout screws, so as to divide the keel into three nearly equal parts. Then add the stem and stern pieces (C, Fig. 2). These are better, probably, when made of green elm. Screw the pieces to the bottom board and bend them, as shown in Fig. 2, by means of a string or wire, fastened to a nail driven into the bottom. Any tough, light wood that is not easily broken when bending will do. Green wood is preferable, because it will retain the shape in which it has been bent better after drying. For the gunwales (a, Fig. 3), procure at a carriage factory, or other place, some light strips of ash, ⅜ inch thick. Nail them to the crossboards and fasten to the end pieces (C) in notches, by several wrappings of annealed iron wire or copper wire, as shown in Fig. 3. Copper wire is better because it is less apt to rust. For fastening the gunwales to the crossboards use nails instead of screws, because the nails are not apt to loosen and come out. The ribs, which are easily made of long, slender switches of osier willow or similar material, are next put in, but before doing this, two strips of wood (b, Fig. 3) should be bent and placed as in Fig. 3. They are used only temporarily as a guide in putting in the ribs, and are not fastened, the elasticity of the wood being sufficient to cause them to retain their position. The osiers may average a little more than ½ inch in thickness and should be cut, stripped of leaves and bark, and put in place while green and fresh. They are attached to the bottom by means of shingle nails driven through holes previously made in them with an awl, and are then bent down until they touch the strips of ash (b, Fig. 3), and finally cut off even with the tops of the gunwales, and notched at the end to receive them (B, Fig. 4). Between the crossboards the ribs are placed at intervals of 2 or 3 inches, while in other parts they are as much as 5 or 6 inches apart. The ribs having all been fastened in place as described, the loose strips of ash (b, Fig. 3) are withdrawn and the framework will appear somewhat as in Fig. 1. In order to make all firm and to prevent the ribs from changing position, as they are apt to do, buy some split cane or rattan, such as used for making chair bottoms, and, after soaking it in water for a short time to render it soft and pliable, wind it tightly around the gunwales and ribs where they join, and also interweave it among the ribs in other places, winding it about them and forming an irregular network over the whole frame. Osiers probably make the best ribs, but twigs of some other trees, such as hazel or birch, will answer nearly as well. For the ribs near the middle of the boat, twigs 5 or 6 feet long are required. It is often quite difficult to get these of sufficient thickness throughout, and so, in such cases, two twigs may be used to make one rib, fastening the butts side by side on the bottom board, and the smaller ends to the gunwales, as before described. In drying, the rattan becomes very tight and the twigs hard and stiff.

The framework is now complete and ready to be covered. For this purpose buy about 18 yards of very strong wrapping paper. It should be smooth on the surface, and very tough, but neither stiff nor very thick. Being made in long rolls, it can be obtained in almost any length desired. If the paper be 1 yard wide, it will require about two breadths to reach around the frame in the widest part. Cut enough of the roll to cover the frame and then soak it for a few minutes in water. Then turn the frame upside down and fasten the edges of the two strips of paper to it, by lapping them carefully on the underside of the bottom board and tacking them to it so that the paper hangs down loosely on all sides. The paper is then trimmed, lapped, and doubled over as smoothly as possible at the ends of the frame, and held in place by means of small clamps. It should be drawn tight along the edges, trimmed and doubled down over the gunwale, where it is firmly held by slipping the strips of ash (b) just inside of the gunwales into notches, which should have been cut at the ends of the crossboards. The shrinkage caused by the drying will stretch the paper tightly over the framework. When thoroughly dry, varnish inside and out with asphaltum varnish thinned with turpentine, and as soon as that has soaked in, apply a second coat of the same varnish, but with less turpentine; and finally cover the laps or joints of the paper with pieces of muslin stuck on with thick varnish. Now remove the loose strips of ash and put on another layer of paper, fastening it along the edge of the boat by replacing the strips as before. When the paper is dry, cover the laps with muslin as was done with the first covering. Then varnish the whole outside of the boat several times until it presents a smooth shining surface. Then take some of the split rattan and, after wetting it, wind it firmly around both gunwales and inside strip, passing it through small holes punched in the paper just below the gunwale, until the inside and outside strips are bound together into one strong gunwale. Then put a piece of oilcloth in the boat between the crossboards, tacking it to the bottom board. This is done to protect the bottom of the boat.

Now you may already have a canoe that is perfectly watertight, and steady in the water, if it has been properly constructed of good material. If not, however, in a few days you may be disappointed to find that it is becoming leaky. Then the best remedy is to cover the whole boat with unbleached muslin, sewed at the ends and tacked along the gunwales. Then tighten it by shrinking and finally give it at least three coats of a mixture of varnish and paint. This will doubtless stop the leaking entirely and will add but little to either the weight or cost.

Rig the boat with wooden or iron rowlocks (B, B, Fig. 5), preferably iron, and light oars. You may put in several extra thwarts or cross-sticks, fore and aft, and make a movable seat (A, Fig. 5). With this you will doubtless find your boat so satisfactory that you will make no more changes.

For carrying the boat it is convenient to make a sort of short yoke (C, Fig. 5), which brings all the weight upon the shoulders, and thus lightens the labor and makes it very handy to carry.

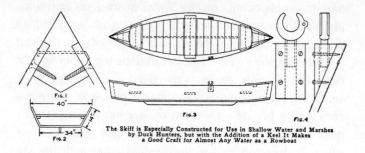

Fig.1
40"

Fig.2
34"

Fig.3

Fig.4

The Skiff is Especially Constructed for Use in Shallow Water and Marshes by Duck Hunters, but with the Addition of a Keel It Makes a Good Craft for Almost Any Water as a Rowboat

# HOW TO BUILD A SKIFF

The following is a description of an easily constructed 12-foot skiff, suitable for rowing and paddling. This is the type used by many duck hunters, as it may be easily pushed through marshes. It is constructed of 3/4-inch dressed pine, or cypress.

The sides consist of planks, 14 inches wide, but 12-inch planks may be used, the length being 12 feet 4 inches. Two stem pieces are constructed as shown in Fig. 1, and the plank ends are fastened to them with screws. Nail a crosspiece on the plank edges in the exact center, so as to space the planks 34 inches apart, as shown in Fig. 2; then turn it over and nail another crosspiece in the center of the planks for width, and make the spacing of the other edges 40 inches. Plane the lower edges so that, in placing a board across them, the surfaces will be level. The floorboards are 6 inches wide and fastened on crosswise, being careful to apply plenty of red lead between all joints and using galvanized nails, 2 inches long.

A deck, 18 inches long, is fastened on each end, as shown in Fig. 3. It is made of strips fastened to a crosspiece. The seats, or thwarts, consist of 10-inch boards, and are placed on short strips fastened to the side planks about 5 inches from the bottom. The oarlocks are held in a wedge-shaped piece of wood, having a piece of gas pipe in them for a bush-ing, the whole being fastened at the upper edge of the side planks with screws, as shown in Fig. 4. The location of these must be determined by the builder.

Some caulking may be required between the bottom, or floor, boards, if they are not nailed tightly against one another. The caulking material may be loosely woven cotton cord, which is well forced into the seams. The first coat of paint should be of red lead mixed with raw linseed oil, and when dry any color may be applied for the second coat.

While, for use in shallow water, these boats are not built with a keel, one can be attached to prevent the boat from "sliding off" in a side wind or when turning around. When one is attached, it should be ¾ inch thick, 3 inches wide, and about 8 feet long.

—B. Francis Dashiell

## HOW TO BUILD AN ICE BOAT AND CATAMARAN

This combination is produced by using the regular type of ice boat and substituting boats for the runners, to make the catamaran.

In constructing the ice boat, use two poles, or timbers, one 16 feet and the other 10½ feet long, crossed at a point 2½ feet from one end of the longer timber. The crossed pieces are firmly braced with wires, as shown.

The mast, which should be about 12 feet long, is set into a mortise cut in the long timber, 15 inches from the front end, and is further stabilized by wires, as shown. A jib boom, about 6 feet long, as well as a main boom, which is 11½ feet long, are hung on the mast in the usual manner.

The front runners consist of band-iron strips, 18 inches long, 3 inches wide, and ⅛ inch thick, with one edge ground like the edge of a skate, and the ends rounding, which are fastened with bolts to the side of wood pieces, 18 inches long, 6 inches wide, and 2 inches thick, allowing the ground edge to project about 1 inch.

When the ice-boat frame is made of poles, the runners are attached to a piece of wood, 12 inches long, shaped as shown and fastened at right angles with bolts running through the shouldered part diagonally. This makes a surface on which the pole end rests and where it is securely fastened with bolts. If squared timbers are used, the runners can be fastened directly to them. The rear, or guiding, runner is fastened between two pieces of wood, so that its edge projects; then it is clamped in a bicycle fork, which should be cut down so that about 3 inches of the forks remain. A hole is bored through the rear end of the long pole to receive the fork head, the upper end of which is supplied with a lever. The lever is attached to the fork head by boring a hole through the lever end at a slight angle to fit the head, allowing sufficient end to be slotted, whereupon a hole is bored through the width of the handle, and a bolt inserted to act as a clamp.

A board is fastened on two crosspieces mortised in the upper part of the pole, for a place to sit on when driving the boat. The sail can be constructed of any good material to the dimensions given.

To rig up the ice boat for use as a catamaran, place a pole across the stern, the length of the pole being equal to the one used on the front part of the ice boat. Two watertight boats are constructed, 16 feet long, 12 inches wide, and 10 inches deep at the center. To make these two boats procure six boards, 16 feet long, 10 inches wide, and 1 inch thick. Three boards are used to make each boat. Bend one board so that it will be in an arc of a circle, then nail on the two side boards, after which the edges of the sides are cut away to the

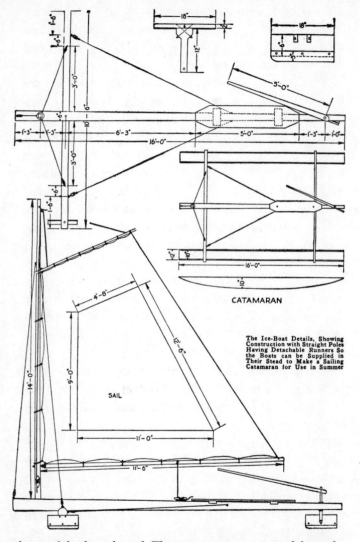

CATAMARAN

The Ice-Boat Details, Showing
Construction with Straight Poles
Having Detachable Runners So
the Boats can be Supplied in
Their Stead to Make a Sailing
Catamaran for Use in Summer

SAIL

shape of the bent board. The runners are removed from the
ice boat, and the boats fastened to the pole ends. A rudder is
attached in the place of the rear, or guiding, runner. The tops
of the boats, or floats, can be covered and made watertight.

# Appendix II:
# Cabins and How to Make Them

Here are some simple directions for making a log cabin which have proved successful on a number of occasions.

The main thing about a cabin is to have proper material—straight logs with as little taper as possible—and to be handy with the ax.

Many have constructed this type of cabin far from a sawmill or any other means of obtaining sawn lumber and have been able to make the cabin with no other tools than the ax and occasionally the saw. The principle is to so notch the logs that they will fit together at the corners, making a tight joint. This is rather a ticklish job.

There is another method of putting up a log cabin that depends upon the availability of a few pieces of inch lumber that may not be more than 6 inches wide and need not be surfaced, i.e., planed.

## Starting the Job

Let's decide that our cabin is to be 8 × 10 feet with a door 2 feet 6 inches wide in the gable end, which faces the south, and that the roof projects 4 feet over this side. This gives the cabin a much more attractive appearance and adds to the protection. Let us make the cabin 6 feet high at the wall and 7 feet, 6 inches high from floor to ridgepole, which will give the roof slightly less than one-half pitch. We will need an accurate measure (a good tape will do), a sharp ax, and a hatchet; two saws—a five-foot crosscut, rigged for two sawyers, and a hand saw—about five pounds of 10-penny nails, and a hammer.

It may be assumed that the cabin is to be constructed somewhere in the land of the pointed fir and that there is available a supply of logs averaging 7 inches at the small end and having a minimum of taper, by which it is meant that the difference in diameters of each end of a given log is very slight.

## Careful About Site

Having selected a site for the cabin on level ground near water, but not so near that a possible flood will carry it away (as I have known to happen), a set of logs, the largest that have been obtained, should be laid in trenches about 6 inches deep, following the floor plan, a rectangle 8 × 10 feet. This serves as an underpinning, makes the cabin warmer, and prevents small animals from gaining a too easy access.

Of the inch lumber already mentioned ten pieces, two for the door frame and eight for the corners, should be cut, 6 feet in length. Place two of them so that the edge of one over-laps the edge of the other and nail securely. You have some-thing that looks like an old-fashioned hog trough without the ends. Make four of them. These "boxes" form the corners of the cabin and avoid the necessity of the difficult notching.

These boxes are placed upright on the foundation, nailed edge inward, and as the logs, accurately cut to fit between them, are placed one upon another, nails are driven through the ends of the boxes into the ends of logs, thus binding the structure together and holding it securely. The doorframe is put in, in like manner.

When the cabin is finished, a small log may be set up in each of the boxes and wedged or nailed into place. This covers the rough boards and gives the cabin the desirable rustic finish. A window 18 × 18 inches may be placed in each side.

## The Roof

The method of building up the gable ends and setting in the roof poles may be best understood from the accompanying diagram. It is evident that lighter logs or poles may be used in the roof, which may be extended over the door more than 4 feet. Six feet would not be too much, as this porch effect may be roughly enclosed on either side, making an excellent place to stack up firewood should the cabin be occupied in winter.

There are roofs and there are roofs. The great point of similarity is their ability to leak. If more lumber is available, by all means put on a board roof and cover it with tarred paper.

The roof *au naturel* is best made by splitting a number of smaller logs, which have been cut long enough to extend 18 or 20 inches beyond the top of the wall, and with a sharp hatchet, hollowing out the split surface on the order of an eaves trough. Place one set on the roof, hollowed face up, nailing it to the roof poles, and place another set with the hollowed face down. This will run off most of the water.

Unless a board floor is used, the dirt of the floor should be scooped out and replaced with 3 or 4 inches of gravel. The unavoidable cracks between the logs may be stopped or "chinked" with moss and mud, but cement is better.

A much better looking and more serviceable cabin will result if care is taken in selecting the logs from straight young trees free from limbs and of uniform size. If possible, cut the logs and let them season thoroughly before putting them into a cabin.

—R. F. McMurry

# Index